To:

Gwen

From:

Charina

Come and Sit for a While

Bench time pondering

Joanna Fruhauf

Come and Sit for a While
©2019 by Joanna Fruhauf
ISBN: 978-0-359-56628-0

Published by Lulu Press, NYC.

Printed and bound in USA.

A few simple thank-you's go out to Corinne Engel and Elisabeth Warner. Thank you for the help and encouragement to finish and fine tune each piece. You ladies are a blessing!

Come and Sit for a While

Bench time pondering

I pray as you read these passages, short testimonies and scenarios, you will move into a deeper relationship with the Lord Jesus Christ. Spend a little time bench side with God. Ask Him to share His heart with you. Listen to the whispers you'll only hear in a close relationship. I see only in part, and I look forward to the day when I will see more clearly. Until then, I will continue to ponder the Word of God, and hold it dear within my heart, allowing it to correct, instruct, encourage and commission me to live more worthy of Him who has called me.

Ponder with me...
Joanna Fruhauf

*"In addition to being a wise man, the Preacher also taught the people knowledge; and he **pondered**, searched out and arranged many proverbs.*

Ecclesiastes 12:9 (NASB)

"Compelling and impacting."
"Like listening to the History Channel, Discovery Channel and Comedy Central all-in-one"

"Dynamic Scriptural insight for everyday life!"

"She speaks with authority, captivating everyone's heart, mind, and spirit!"

Joanna Fruhauf is an author, speaker, singer/songwriter, recording artist and lead singer of the band, Gracious Vine. She speaks at women's events, churches, retreats, and conferences around the country.

Joanna got saved in 1974 at the tender age of 11. Her mother's mentor poured into and challenged her to learn the Scriptures, search them out and be a fully involved member of the adult Bible studies at her young age. It cultivated a passion and learning of the Scriptures that continues to this day.

Years later, as a young mother, she opened her home, teaching Bible studies and hosting prayer groups, always encouraging others to dig deeper, broadening their understanding of the heart of God through His word.

Joanna has worked her adult life in the non-profit field, supporting ministries and helping to develop long-range processes and growth. She also has been involved in leadership positions of local, national and international Christian organizations, like Concerned Women for America and International Cops for Christ.

Her messages are passionate, intriguing, a mix of everyday life, science, and Scriptures, with a splash of humor. As some have said, they are "a mix of the Bible Channel, History Channel,

Discovery Channel, and Comedy Central all in one talk." Each element helps the listener relate to a modern context and application of God's authoritative word, and each message is crafted to fit a theme, often with talking points for break-out sessions when requested.

Having Joanna speak at your next event will prove to be a most exciting and encouraging time for you and your group. Speaking engagements with Joanna include time to develop relationships, forge ahead into new ground, and inspire others to maximize their strengths while minimizing their weaknesses in a Christ-centered and focused message.

If you choose to have the Gracious Vine perform at your event, they will entertain your audience with rich melodies and passionate vocals that will inspire the spirit and soul of every audience member.

For booking and more information:

www.GraciousVine.com

GraciousVine@gmail.com

CONTENTS

Too Busy

And Jesus answered and said to her, "Martha, Martha, you are worried and troubled about many things."
Luke 10:41

As a kid, I can remember watching a television program that fascinated me. There was a man on a variety show spinning plates. He started by spinning one plate on top of a thin wooden pole and continued to add poles and dishes across the stage until there were at least ten. I was amazed as he continued to race around the stage, back and forth, keeping the plates atop their poles by stroking them and quick to help the ones that were starting to wobble. I was mesmerized by it all. What agility, what discipline, what speed and ability! It was a talent! It was fun!

Not too long ago, it struck me how I am just like that plate spinner, always running around, ever mindful of things that need tending. However, instead of it being a talent, this time it was an indictment of a life a bit too busy. I often say I am a "Mary" in a "Martha" body. I enjoy the ability to do as much as I can. I get a rush being creative. I am thrilled with a sense of accomplishment, even if only for my satisfaction. Psychologists say that most people are happier when they are busy, and busyness makes me happy.

I don't often like to sit; I want to "do." I will sit from time to time, but before I know it, I'm adding plates. There have been a few times when plates have fallen off and crashed to the floor, shattering in pieces, and yet I grab more plates.

Cindy, an original member of the band Gracious Vine, posted on Facebook what prompted the CD project, *Come & Sit for a While*: a picture of an empty bench. The caption read, "Come and sit a while." I was transfixed. The image seemed to grab hold of my heart and mind and forced me to stop for a moment and hear the voice of God compelling, convicting, and compassionately calling me to join Him at the bench. At that moment, I recalled the plate spinner. I was rebuked for not having spent quality time with the Lord in weeks and was compelled to stop everything and answer the call to sit for a while with Him.

It was rejuvenating, refreshing, relaxing and reconstructive. Corrected, I realized, God is the source of my strength, my energies, my creativity, my anchor, and my balance. It is in time spent with Him that I am reinvigorated for the tasks ahead of me. I am comforted that I can bring to Him my frustrations, my pride, my compulsion, my obsessions, and busyness.

What plates can you put down, even if only for a moment, to spend time with Him at the bench?

Greatest Invitation

"Come and let us reason together," says the Lord.
Isaiah 1:18a

Can you think about that for a moment? The God of the universe, the One who set every law of physics into play, created the world, and brought forth every creature, invites us to join him in a discussion. He has welcomed us to "reason together" with Him. How amazing is that? What a beautiful invitation, and what a fantastic privilege!

This open table is a tremendous opportunity to respond to God. It's as if I can hear God saying, "Bring your cards to the table. What's in your hand? Do you have questions? Do you have fears? Do you wrestle with My commands, My instructions, My directives or corrections? Are you willing to hear Me when you come? Are you willing to lay down your struggles, regrets, and worries? Will you be willing to give up your wants, sins, and pride? What have they produced in and through you? Have they made you stronger, given you purpose, changed your life for the better?"

This holy invitation comes exclusively from the God of Abraham, Isaac, Jacob, and Joseph. There is no other offer like this from any other god in any of the world religions. Not one! It is the exclusive offer of the God who created all things, of the God who created you.

The invitation stands. It is there for whosoever would be willing to engage the Lord in dialogue, to spend the time with Him, learning of Him and submitting to Him. We need to stop the scurrying that keeps us so preoccupied and distracted by our own lives. We need to surrender, bringing our questions, concerns, and failures. It's in responding to this invitation that we learn to set things in order, instead of scampering around. Having some special, one on one time with the Lord, whether at a bench or around a decision table where we can hash out our arguments, fears, doubts, and pain. The God of all creation invites us to the table, so we can receive His love, compassion and purpose for us.

God is not put off by our inadequacies; instead, He seeks to make use of them. The only times He can't is when we pretend they don't exist or refuse to submit them to His authority. We need to be fully willing to dialogue with God and wrestle with things God has instructed or corrected us about, ready to take on His understandings. Then we will walk following His desires, and will be more fully equipped for every good work that He permits and commissions.

Spend some time today, this week, this month pondering what God might say about those cards you hold so close to your chest. He sees them, and He knows them. You can't hide them from Him. As you lay them down before Him, you'll come to hear His voice as He beckons you deeply, loves you unconditionally, and genuinely cares about who you are and where you are going.

Pure Driven Snow

Though your sins are like scarlet,
I will make them white as snow.
Isaiah 1:18b

A few years ago, my daughter shared a tender story of a little
toddler leaving a store with her father. It was a bright and brisk
winter day. Everyone was catching up on their Christmas
shopping after a massive snowfall. This father navigated through
the drifts and piles of snow in the yet uncleared parking lot with
his children, the youngest daughter firmly in hand. She was
distracted, looking around at all the mountainous heaps of pure
white snow. Then, my daughter overheard the most adorable
question. The little girl pointed and asked, "Daddy, why are
there sparkles in the snow?"

Well, that was it! Our hearts melted away due to the precious
purity, innocence and wonder of the question. Everyone in the
room had the same response: "Awww!"

I can't tell you how the father answered, what his response was,
or if his heart melted as ours did. I can tell you that he looked at
her with a smile and put her in the car. Would she even have
understood a logical answer to the question at that tender age?

The next few weeks were cold enough to keep the snow around
till long after all the Christmas trees got tossed to the curb. We
had several snowfalls that fell that year. Each one came just in

time to cover up the messy and dirty snow from the previous storm. Each new blanket refreshed the landscape, making it beautiful once again.

The constant storms that winter got me pondering the snow's beauty. I love the way the snow changes the landscape, dampens the noise and quiets the environment. I find it fascinating that each snowflake is unique, with no two alike, much like our fingerprints, DNA, or retina scans. That's just amazing to me. It brought to mind my favorite Scripture, Isaiah 1:18, which says, "'Come now and let us reason together,'" says the Lord, 'Though your sins are as scarlet, I will make them white as snow ...'"

God has an incredible ability to change the landscape in our lives if we come to Him with our concerns, cares, and cries. He is uniquely able to deaden the noises that overwhelm and consume us.

With each snow cover, He makes the environment we are in beautiful, and with each snowflake a unique word of love. The snow may fall gently, quietly, forcing us to listen intently to His individual words of love for us. Each word, overcoming our circumstance and transforming where we live into a land of wonder and purity. Each snowflake unique, each spoken word from His throne loving us.

When the storm has passed, and the Sun is shining, we see sparkles in the snow; glistening rays of hope. Each unique word from heaven sparkles with a unique splendor, beauty, and significance in our lives.

Where does your life need a covering of pure white snow?
Think about how different the landscape of your life would look
if you would let Him change it and purify it.

Open Your Treasures

And when they had opened their treasures,
they presented gifts to Him: gold, frankincense, and myrrh.
Matthew 2:11

I don't know about you but the Magi that came to Bethlehem
intrigue me. We always relegate this story to Christmas, but our
lives are full, day in, day out with gold, frankincense, and myrrh.
In looking a little closer at the Scripture itself, two things jump
out at me. First, "They opened their treasures." What treasures?
Wasn't it just the three items? The word alone, "treasures,"
indicates an incredible wealth, an abundance of items, lavish and
overflowing.

Secondly, the delineated items of gold, frankincense, and myrrh
caused some thoughts to stir in me. These items certainly must
have greater significance than the actual physical elements,
which I have little or none to speak of myself. If I were one of
the Magi, what would my gold, frankincense or myrrh gifts be
today?

Gold is, of course, rare and extremely valuable. It can withstand
fire and acids, it does not tarnish, and it is pliable. In mining for
gold today, it takes acres and acres of land to produce one gold
bar. It is the gift of Kings and the currency of kingdoms. All
true crowns of victory or kingship have been made from gold.

What are the crowns in my life that I bring to Jesus in humble submission? We all have strengths, gifts or talents. What have we done well? Is it a relationship we have secured over time that needed repair, a long-lasting marriage, a job well done? Purity guarded? Victories won? Healing received? From where have our achievements and successes come? Different aptitudes, talents, and gifts, whether artistic or logical, can all be given back to Jesus, recognizing that it was His upholding power that secured us through the sorting, sifting and purifying fires that produced that gold in us.

As well as gold, frankincense and myrrh, too, are secured through a strenuous process. Created from a resin which is excreted from special trees, farmers intentionally wound the trees and allow the sap to dry into "tears". Harvesters, cut the tree's bark deeply, and the tree oozes out its life-sap. Sap tears build up and run down the side of the tree's bark, are left to dry out and then are harvested. In ancient times, these rare resins were used for medicinal purposes and in religious practices. At various times in history, both frankincense and myrrh were worth their weight in gold.

What are the things in my life that have cost me? Where have I suffered loss? Where was there a great sacrifice, or where did hurt leave a mark, drawing out of me my life at times, leaving tears and scars?

Frankincense is used as a sweet fragrance often in a religious ceremony, while myrrh is bitter and was used frequently in burials. I wondered in what areas my heart had to reconcile these different types of sacrifices and hurts. Perhaps an area when I have incurred a cost for the benefit of another as a sacrifice on their behalf, or without reciprocation giving myself away at a loss for someone else to grow. What about the times I have willingly taken a personal hit and undergone pain, discipline or malicious wounds from others? These painful times must be brought to the Lord and surrendered, allowing the healing and comforting of God to then be turned around and used for the benefit of someone else. I had not thought of those areas in my life as treasures, and yet, apparently, they are treasures once they are submitted to Christ. He can take what others mean for harm and turn it into good! What hope, what healing, what joy everlasting!

Then, there are the burials. How many things have I longed for, hoped for, dreamed of or pursued, that had died? How many pains and hurts do we tuck away, never to see the light of day, let alone the Light of Christ? These also, must be brought before the Lord and surrendered. All of our pain can be healed, and from ashes, beauty can come, life and strength. It rises as incense before the Lord.

When was the last time you brought all your treasures, these unique and complex treasures, to Him, and opened them all up, making them all available to Him to use in a manner in which He sees as fit and proper? God can use and wants access to our treasures; our gold, frankincense and myrrh, our trophies, triumphs, failures, sacrifices, and wounds. They are all very precious in His sight. They are all deep within our heart's storehouse; acquired at great personal cost and sacrifice. Whether they are our trophies or our tears, God wants them all.

Transformation

And do not be conformed to this world, but be transformed by the renewing of your mind, that you may prove what is that good and acceptable and perfect will of God.
Romans 12:2

Have you ever been involved in a project that involved completely renovating a room, house, or environment? For years I have enjoyed television shows that remodel homes. I loved watching *Trading Spaces* and *Extreme Makeover* on the HGTV network. The first show was a fun, light-hearted exchange of rooms between friends. Each would do the other's home, trusting just enough to relinquish the control of decorating one single room to a friend or family member. People have a tough time trying to translate their hearts desires to others, and the interpretation of it in artistic expression may not be what the individual wanted. It might not have end with what they had hoped. However, it was merely a room, conformed to fit into a budget and style with minor surface changes.

Then there was *Extreme Makeover*, where someone's home needed an upgrade. When the team of experts came, they would completely knock down and remove the old house and replace it with a completely redesigned, brand new home. It was a show that grabbed you by the gut, brought tears to your eyes and left you emotionally moved and inspired. It was transformative; it was radical, it was complete, and it was all or nothing. The renovators completely took away all remnants of the previous dwelling, leaving nothing and, eventually, all new and nothing like before. It provided a clean slate, a new start, a fresh beginning and, a potential for growth within those new walls. In both shows, people trusted their home with someone else. Each homeowner had trust in either their friends and family or the experts.

Most of us believe people, to an extent, but we feel we can do a much better job, and so we want to control. We've had people fail us before, so our expectation is low, or we place unreasonable expectations on people to do what they cannot, so we walk away disappointed. We reflect that same level of trust in God. not entirely giving Him full authority to do whatever He deems necessary and useful. We limit His ability to work in our lives and therefore only have small changes in our walk with Him. Yet, He alone makes us new in a completely radical way.

A complete transformation is the type of change God wants with us. Too often we as believers will only give Jesus the creative right to one room of our lives and heart, and even though we ask Him to come in and make adjustments, we demand that the changes meet specific criteria. Often believers are unhappy with the results because they weren't what they envisioned.

Are we willing to take a good look at the "house" we've built? Are we ready for the radical transformation that He alone has the power, authority, and expertise to provide? It's not until we completely take ourselves out of the equation and let Him have His way that we will see real transformation and actual change.

Fishers of Men

Then He said to them, "Follow Me, and I will make you fishers of men." They immediately left their nets and followed Him. Matthew 4:19-20

Have you ever gone fishing? The largest fish I ever caught was a small three-inch sunfish in a pond at a campground when I was fifteen. My husband enjoys fishing, and I enjoy just watching him, sitting in a chair beachside with a book in hand, or watching him come home with his prizes and our dinner! He has gone surf casting, on charter boats, and even river fishing. My son literally takes fishing to a different level; he fishes below the surface, swimming underwater as he goes spearfishing.

Have you seen the show, *The Deadliest Catch*? The men use either huge nets or what they call pots. With these, they can fill the bellies of their boats in short order. It is the network that equips them to catch many with fewer hands. Imagine trying to fill the belly of one of those boats with individual fishing poles. The energies expended would be counterproductive.

God's Word talks to us about fishing. He calls us fishers of men. Interestingly, every time I, my husband, my son, or even most of my friends have gone fishing, they are only able to capture one fish at a time.

Jesus uses this moment in Matthew 4 to show that to haul in the big catches, we need to work together. Like a net, everyone needs to help, supporting and working in unison. It isn't a one-man, one-pole mentality. God loves teams. He works through the joint effort of many. As our lives interconnect, intermingle, and interweave with other believers, we can bring many into the Kingdom of God. One may sow, one may water, and another may reap, all the while knowing the increase comes from God Himself.

There are always those times and opportunities where we may stand alone on a shore or dock with a single pole, a word or prayer for someone that can help to lead them to Christ, but more often than not, God wants us working in unity, as a team.

As we join hands with each other, creating that network, we help to catch others, less fall by the wayside, through the cracks and plummet into desperate places. There is no more significant opportunity to bring healing, no greater hope than when brothers and sisters dwell together in unity.

Where can you put your hand? Where are you being called to help pull in the nets, clean them, work them, or mend them? Consider where in the boat you are invited to participate and get more fully engaged, without regard for yourself, but looking toward the waters as they teem with lives in desperate need for *Him*! Then, pull them in.

My Betrothed

*"I will betroth you to Me forever; Yes, I will betroth you to Me
In righteousness and justice, In lovingkindness and mercy;"
Hosea 2:19*

So much of the Bible uses word pictures, whether told in story
form or lived out in principle by individuals. There are so many
to choose from, and yet one continues to repeat through the
entirety of Scripture: marriage. This sacred and holy union,
blessed by God between a man and a woman, is where physical
intimacy consummates the wedding for the unique purpose of
creating a robust, stable and positive environment. In this setting,
children can be raised, nurtured and fortified in character, mind,
and spirit. Our creator designed no other environment for such a
purpose.

Now, does this mean that all marriages are perfect? No, far from
it. All humans are incredibly flawed in character and nature.
Do failed marriages prove the model doesn't work? No, not by
any means! Rather, they more fully display man's desperate need
for the real example.

From the very beginning of the Bible, marriage, a covenant
between one man and one woman, was supposed to set the tone
for the type of relationship we are to have with God. This type
of relationship is where He has done whatever it takes to secure
the safety and the well-being of His Beloved. Love is returned in
respect, honor, and fidelity.

There is a beckoning that goes on before we come to a full understanding of that type of relationship with God. First, there is a winning over of the heart, a wooing of the spirit. It is the great Love of God, which He has for us, that draws us to Him. He desires that we would come to a place of repentance, that we might recognize our desperate need for a redeemer, a savior, a master, and lord. We need Someone that will guide us and captivate our hearts, teaching us, sharing with us, calling out to us, and drawing us into a new place, a deeper relationship with Him.

Have you heard the call of God to your heart? Do you recognize that He loves you and desires to have a long-term covenant with you? Do you want an intimate relationship with God? Are you willing to pay a price of fidelity in spirit, soul and body for Him?

Just like a successful marriage between a man and a woman, we need to be willing to trust, submit to, and obey God. When we do, our reward is great, and the cherishing and nurturing that flows towards us is more than we could ever hope or imagine.

The Radiance of Purity

"Come now, and let us reason together,"
Says the Lord, "Though your sins are like scarlet,
They shall be as white as snow;
Though they are red like crimson,
They shall be as wool."
Isaiah 1:18

Consider this: you are standing in a chapel, a guest of your dear friend, the groom. You are excited to see the one he loves, someone he sacrificed so much for. You know she has a broken past, but you know too that his vast estate and influence have the ability to wipe that slate clean for her. The chapel is adorned with fragrant flowers, light flooding in through amazing high multi-panel arched windows, guests dressed to the nines, and the groom standing, eagerly waiting for the appearing of his bride. The musical ensemble plays a sweet harmonious ballad.

Suddenly, trumpets blare, announcing her entrance. You turn to the rear of the church, hearing the doors open wide. Without hesitation, everyone stands to their feet in anticipation of the groom's bride.

She steps over the threshold. Everyone gasps, seeing her white dress a tattered, torn and filthy mess. She walks in with a soiled, stained and putrid-smelling garment. Her hair and skin, dirty, unwashed and caked with soil from a lifestyle of gutter living.

She passes aisle after aisle of guests with stunned faces, shocked
that she did nothing in preparation for the groom.
How repulsed are you thinking about it? It is so contrary to what
we hope for and expect to see for the groom we know and love.

Can we be honest? Sin is ugly and repugnant.

If we had eyes to see just how horrible it is in the scheme of life
and eternity, we would be mortified and humbled by our sins.
Even the small ones we currently justify.

We expect a bride, because of her great love for the groom, to
ready herself, to present herself as pure and holy as she can on
the most important day. Why would the Lord expect less from
His bride, you and me? Do we justify our sin, and continue to
walk around in filthy clothes, unwashed, unprepared for His
coming? Using excuses, "Well that's who I am, I can't change,
take it or leave it," assumes we can abuse and take advantage of
His love.

God desires that we walk washed, cleansed, and purified by His
love, mercy, and forgiveness. He wants His bride to be radiant,
clean, pure, holy, spotless, without blemish and white as snow.
Jesus made provision for that with His blood. The sacrifice was
so intense, so complete and immeasurable, that once the bride
recognized what was accomplished on her behalf, how He
ransomed her life with His own from an evil taskmaster and
secured her freedom with His authority, she would willingly
surrender her past and walk in newness of His life.

His blood, purchased her freedom, her cleansing, and her future. It paid the price for her sin, and she is made white and pure, but that does not mean she can continue in the behaviors He redeemed her from.

If the body of Christ would consider the above image of the bride and choose to make herself ready, then the world would once again recognize the freedom she has, the beauty of her relationship, the purity of her heart, and the fidelity of her love and desire to live a life that pleases her groom. Perhaps the world would be stirred even jealous to become a radiant bride along with the Church.

We need to recognize that, though His love is great and His gift of salvation is freely given, there is responsibility on our part to repent of our sins, our gutter glories, and seek to live a life that would be pleasing to the groom, to become a bride worthy of Him, without spot or blemish.

Dwelling in the Father's Tent

"And Bezalel and Aholiab, and every gifted artisan in whom the Lord has put wisdom and understanding, to know how to do all manner of work for the service of the sanctuary, shall do according to all that the Lord has commanded."
Exodus 36:1

In reading about the construction of the Tabernacle of Moses, we find that two people in particular were commissioned with the crafting and building of the furniture and structure. It was a daunting task. Not only were they working with tremendous amounts of gold, silver, and bronze, building a sanctuary for a God that frightened them on the mountain, but they were building a sanctuary for a God that wiped out their enemies and destroyed a country that held them captive.

God was showing Himself as powerful, holy, and sovereign, and He even gave them a personal warning to build it precisely as Moses had seen it on the mountaintop. If they did not do this, they would die. No pressure, right? That job sounds terrifyingly complex. Not only is the end result detailed and specific; the temptation around all those precious metals and gems would have been difficult to quell.

God seems so strict, so harsh, so mean and calloused to me. How do you fulfill such a task? How do you get the exact interpretation of someone else's viewpoint without making a mess of it (We've all played Telephone!)?

I researched these men. I found in Hebrew, the name Bezalel means, *in the shadow of God*, and the name Aholiab means, *in the tent of the father*. These men had a very intimate, personal relationship with God. Their names indicate that they were close enough to God to see beyond what others might perceive as harsh and judgmental. They saw Him as holy and sovereign. They were in close enough proximity to see the full outline of God's shadow themselves, to be in His shadow personally, to inhabit the tent of the father, hearing His whispers, His heartbeat, His heart's cry, and recognizing shadows and silhouettes of His character.

Are we staying close in God's shadow? Are we personally close enough to encounter it? Are we dwelling within the tent of the Father enough to be taught and corrected, and to peacefully enjoy His presence? Or are we clamoring with all those outside, busy, distracted, and avoiding the intimate fellowship that may expose our heart to His?

Are we willing to be close enough to be instructed by Him? If not, we can never presume that we will be asked to build anything for Him. As we learn to spend time with Him in the tent—in His shadow—our tears are wiped dry; our cares are shared with Him, our fellowship deepens, and we are more willing to be known by Him. It's there that we come to seek and know Him. Regardless of the storms—the thunder and lightning—we find assurance in an ever-increasing dynamic as deep calls to deep in our hearts, minds, and spirit.

I want God to continue to beckon me to the inner chambers of
His presence. My desire is to be close to Him, hearing the cares
and concerns of His heart, just as much as I want Him to
understand and be concerned with mine. I long to have the back
and forth communication, the heart-to-heart, eye-to-eye
interaction with the Lord. I desire to be acquainted with Him and
the power of His resurrection, to spend time in His tent, close in
His presence. Don't you?

You Are Living Stones

You also, as living stones, are being built up a spiritual house,
a holy priesthood, to offer up spiritual sacrifices acceptable to
God through Jesus Christ.
1 Peter 2:5

What are living stones? How are we equated with that?
Scripturally, living stones have nothing to do with some pseudo-
science or metaphysical energy within certain stones. They have
everything to do with God's Word being alive and growing
within us. Diamonds and all other crystal-based rocks are living
stones because they grow and develop over time through various
processes (once again, not because of any "energy," power, or
life force within them!) They are considered precious and semi-
precious stones. They have value because they form through
processes that are unique, rare and slow. The manner by which
they are unearthed is time-consuming and often treacherous,
which causes their value to increase.

Living stones are comprised of mineral molecules that end up
linking, connecting and interlocking to form a well-organized
structure. Its properties and facets permit the reflecting and
refracting of light as it bounces off or passes through the crystal.

Interestingly, most crystals grow due to either heat, pressure or
deposits. When we think of our walk with God, those elements
are often the very processes that develop us as well. Heat and
pressure seem to burn off the wasteful selfishness of our lives,

leaving behind a simple walk where we are more concerned for His reputation than our own, and a desire to be a good and worthy reflection of His abundant grace, mercy, and love. The deposits of time spent in His Word and presence seem to share with us valuable pieces of His heart, showing us, instructing us, and encouraging us to walk in a manner worthy of Him. Through these factors, He calls us to live lives of obedience to His will at the sacrifice of our whims, wishes, fantasies, lusts, and justifications.

Why does God equate us with living stones and why does He desire this of us? Well, as someone who has been a jewelry designer working with various elements, stones, and precious metals, I can tell you that the counterfeits—the glass, plastic, and man-made items—do not hold the same wonder, value or beauty as the living stones. To the undiscerning eye, they may look the same, but those who work with the items regularly can spot the counterfeit immediately. God doesn't want us to be counterfeits; He wants His house to be built up by the precious, valuable and significantly more beautiful rare stones. Why? *"So that you may proclaim the praises of Him who called you out of darkness into His marvelous light;* (1 Peter 2:9b).

Nothing reflects and refracts light as wonderfully as high-grade natural diamonds. They are the most precious of all "living stones." Man-made glass can't do the light justice, it can display some of the wonder and majesty, but not all.

I don't want to be a counterfeit. I want to be the genuine article. But I also know what that means. Growing slowly, secretly, with heat, pressure and various deposits. Only being willing to interlock with the source, Jesus Christ, am I am then to be the stone and structure He has called me to be. That I might, together with others of like mind, be able to display the manifold (many folds, multiple facets) of God's mercy and grace.

It's with this fascination that I desire to submit my actions, attitudes, and agendas to Him.

Are we willing to endure the process?

Greatest Exchange Policy in The Universe!

For you know the grace of our Lord Jesus Christ, that though
He was rich, yet for your sakes He became poor, that you
through His poverty might become rich.
2 Corinthians 8:9

How many times have you gone shopping in a clothing store,
saw something you liked, tried it on, and then purchased it? All
excited, you took it home, and when the day came that you
wanted to wear it, you were less than happy and wondered what
you were thinking when you first got it.

Come on, ladies! We do this all the time, and fortunately, the
stores generally have a decent policy—within 30 days or so, with
all tags and receipts—where you can bring it back and either get
a refund or an exchange for something better. Whew! Good
thing, right?

But how many of us have worn that item we got, then end up
spilling something on it? For argument's sake let's say, the day
you wore it, your car dies, and you end up walking in the rain,
getting splashed by passing traffic and covered in filthy mud.
Now, try and take that back to the store! Yeah, that will go well.

The Lord Jesus Christ offers us an incredible exchange policy,
where we can come to Him with our failures, our frailty, our
filth, our weaknesses, our disobedience, our rebellions, and our
defiance, and, as we return and repent, we will be washed clean.

Now that doesn't mean that we can then go back to the mud and mess around there. Jesus forgave the adulterous woman, the tax collectors, and prostitutes, but followed His forgiveness and healing by saying, "Go and sin no more." That was not a request; it was a command. It is the responsibility on our part of forgiveness and repentance. The salvation of God is a gift, but it is not cheap. There was a huge cost on God's behalf, and on ours. The cost to us is a life that pleases Him, not ourselves. Too many people think that God turns a blind eye to willful sin that we choose to participate in and practice. The Scriptures do not bear that out.

1 Corinthians 6: 18-20 tells us: *"Flee sexual immorality. Every sin that a man does is outside the body, but he who commits sexual immorality sins against his own body. Or do you not know that your body is the temple of the Holy Spirit who is in you, whom you have from God, and you are not your own? For you were bought at a price; therefore glorify God in your body and in your spirit, which are God's.*

When we get a grasp of what Christ has done for us and secured for us, why would we want to settle for less than what honors Him and makes His heart happy? What a tremendous exchange: my filth for His eternal and unfathomable love and abundant life.

There is no greater exchange policy in the entire universe than the one we can have with God. He recognizes our utter detestable filth, and yet even when caught in the very act of horrific sin, God is willing to extend to us freedom, forgiveness, mercy, and restoration if we will return and repent, as we go and sin no more.

He extends an opportunity for us to lay hold of life eternal and life abundant. This offer is such an amazing, outrageous, extraordinary, ostentatious, loving act of His mercy to those who will return and abide in Him.

"You Are Worth More . . ."

*"Are not five sparrows sold for two copper coins? And not one
of them is forgotten before God. But the very hairs of your head
are all numbered. Do not fear therefore; you are of more value
than many sparrows."*
Luke 12:6-7

Where was the last place you found money? Either a few extra
dollars in one of your pockets from that winter jacket you wore
last year, or the pants that are fitting you again, or a buck on the
sidewalk?

The most significant bill I ever found was a $20 bill. That was
thrilling. I pulled into a parking spot. As I got out of my car,
there, having just cleared my tire was a filthy, wet, tattered and
torn $20 bill. If I remember right, I used my debit card in the
store so that I could still have the bill in my hands because it was
such a cool find.

Finding a tattered and torn, filthy, smelly currency bill was
exciting. But why? Just think of what may have happened to it,
think of all the ways it was driven over, by what and when.
Think of the lack of luster, not as one of the bright, clean, dry,
stiff, crisp bills from the bank.

The reason for the excitement is the inherent value ascribed to it
by the authority of the land, the Federal Reserve and US
government. No other piece of paper found in that deplorable

condition would be striking such excitement in anyone's heart. For this little piece of paper, there would be clicking of heels mid-air! The Federal Reserve ascribed value to that paper, and said it is worth a certain amount. Regardless of the condition it is in, it can be used to purchase goods because of that value. That's an interesting concept.

Let's apply that now to our lives. Ever struggle with your sense of self-worth, your value, your worthiness to God?

Jesus said that God numbers every hair on our head, and that we are worth more than many sparrows. God has ascribed value to us as the creation of His hands, made in His image for His good pleasure. That value is not diminished by what we have been through, what has trampled us down, what has taken advantage of us, or what has happened to us, hurt us, broken us, scarred us or torn us. We still have an incredible value which *He* seeks to redeem and restore. God seeks to reconcile us back to Himself because, as the creation of His hands, He aims to see our worth brought to full form and function.

Value has been ascribed to us and is backed up by His authority. It is a value proven by His actions to redeem us. The price He would be willing to do so, His own life.

The reality is we are weather-beaten, tattered and torn. But similarly, even if you found a 100-dollar bill in a filthy toilet, it still has its value, and it can be reclaimed, washed and used, because the highest authority in the land has ascribed its value. It can be brought to a bank and traded out for a brand-new bill.

So, the next time either you, the enemy of your soul or someone else tries to imply that you have no worth, or are of no value, please remember that God loves you, created you and purposed you!

He has ascribed value to you, paying close attention to your life, even numbering the hairs on your head like a loving, doting father. Scripture tells us clearly that He knew you before the foundations of the earth. In your mother's womb, He knew you and wove together all your inward parts, personality, gifts and purpose.

He proclaims you are worth more than many $100 bills.

A Loud Thunder

After it a voice roars; He thunders with His majestic voice,
And He does not restrain them when His voice is heard.
Job 37:4

Give me a good old thunderstorm any day! I love it: all the
lightning, the clashing, the flashing, and the explosive power that
tears open the sky the torrential downspouts! Rend the heavens,
Lord, and come down!

For years, we've camped on the beaches of Long Island. Without
fail, there is one blustery storm that rolls through, shaking the
trailer, toppling tents, ripping off awnings, overturning some
chairs, and soaking everything. They never disappoint. There is
just something about the majesty, authority and fearsome power
of it all.

Though I love it, I do get startled, jolted, and even apprehensive
at times. I take precautions, using and exercising as much
wisdom as I have. I'd be a fool if it didn't cause me to fear,
knowing the inherent ability that electric power has to destroy,
even kill.

I think of God in these same terms often. I certainly understand
Him to be a loving and doting father, a bold and courageous
defender, the lover of my soul, but I dare not forget that He is
God!

" 'Father, glorify Your name.' Then a voice came from heaven,
saying, 'I have both glorified it and will glorify it again.'
Therefore the people who stood by and heard it said that it had
thundered. Others said, 'An angel has spoken to Him.' Jesus
answered and said, 'This voice did not come because of Me, but
for your sake'" (John 12:28-30).

Toward the end of Jesus' earthly ministry, He made several
mentions of His intended goal: death on a cross for the
redemption, salvation, and reconciliation of humanity to God.
The crowd clamored around him, and naturally, some were
closer than others. At this moment, all were within close enough
proximity to hear the voice of God, but it was discernment was
critical in deciphering the voice of God.

Jesus cried out a prayer to His Father. The response of the voice
from heaven was for the benefit of all present, and yet some
completely missed it.

All they thought they heard was thunder. Some understood it a
little differently, as if an angel said something to Jesus that only
He would understand, and yet some—certainly the writer of the
gospel, John—heard it and *knew* it was a sound from Heaven, the
voice of God that distinctly said, " I have glorified it, and I will
glorify it again."

Why the differences?

I don't think it was merely physical proximity, but perhaps, most
probably, it was spiritual distance.

Indeed, John, Jesus' beloved disciple, a man who had surrendered all, followed fully, and dedicated everything to Jesus, was well aware it was God who said it and what God had said.

It was crystal clear.

The crowd followed Jesus because they recognized He spoke of useful, sensible and beneficial truths that they could apply mentally and practically in their lives, as long as things were convenient and comfortable.

The last group were those who only heard God's voice as if it were thunder. There was no sense of personal attachment to the voice, no semblance of personal interaction with the power and force they heard. These people didn't really follow or appreciate, but watched out of vain curiosity, with no real interest for themselves.

Often, people who are distant from God don't recognize His voice: His heart towards them, His desire and attempts to connect, interact with and engage them in a dialogue. They realize a power or force, perhaps some light from a non-relational power, like an electrical emanating source somewhere in the universe, but not a personal God who wants to love on them and bring them home.

Some people seek the Lord fervently. Others consider faith in God a convenience as long as it is comfortable, fits in with their lifestyle, choices, and justifications. They like the benefits they have by playing what I call the "God" card. But the personal surrender is not there. Many have no desire to be accountable to God. They do not want to have to change their minds; they don't want to stop what they are doing, and they believe the justification they have wrapped their sin up in. These people refuse to walk in an intimate relationship with Jesus and submit their lives, their thoughts, their world view to His authority and wisdom.

Then there are those times that I get it. I hear His voice and I am keenly aware of what He said.

None of us are fully there yet. Sanctification is a process. As we approach Him, we will be able to hear the voice of God clearer, becoming more aware of what He is saying. It is a journey that we choose to walk, one in which we select the depth of that relationship at each encounter.

Are we moving ever deeper, or are we stagnant or distracted and standing at a distance?

I want to move closer. How about you?

Mighty Man of Valor

Then the Lord turned to him and said, "Go in this might of yours, and you shall save Israel from the hand of the Midianites. Have I not sent you?"
Judges 6:14

Poor, poor Gideon. It is a scary thing to be called by God to go and face an enemy, especially one from which you've been hiding. As Christians we hear these stories of courage and strength and we cheer for them. Men and women like Moses, Elijah, Hannah, Sarah, all had so much to combat, so many things pushing against them. We celebrate at the end of the story, getting excited that they were triumphant and victorious, and we are encouraged to see God empower them.

We long to be like them; we desire to have lives that declare and display the glory of God in manners of equal stature.

But wait...

That means we will have to endure, persevere, stand alone, and trust God against all types of difficult situations. I often expect a successful outcome to be swift, painless, and gilded with accolades of our friends, families and fellow believers. I've cowered, terrified, in disbelief that God would call me to have to deal with certain things. I often hope for a swift and easy life, not wanting to deal with conflict. God often calls us to do battle and be counter-cultural. He calls us to be bold, courageous and strong and to trust in His power and authority.

God calls His people to stand for righteousness and against sin. In today's world, hearts grow cold, love waxes hard, and selfish preservation reigns supreme.

Why do we look at movies with heroes and heroines with such admiration, and yet fail to rise to the occasion when we have the opportunity? Why do we think that we would receive from the Lord the same empowerment He gave to the heroes of the faith if we continually shrink back behind the line? Choosing the easy road, the path of least resistance, gains no rewards and creates no heroes, just a generation of sheep led to slaughter.

It is often through stressful, challenging, and even difficult struggles we are rewarded with a victor's crown if we do not shrink back. My mother has often said, "Plants don't grow strong in greenhouses". She's right. The plant needs the wind to buffet it, so that its core becomes resilient and strong. It needs to send roots deep into the ground, securing itself from winds, storms and droughts. It can't do that in a greenhouse. Those elements and opportunities are missing in an easy environment.

Remember, it was only Peter that walked on water. Why? There were several other disciples in the boat, but they did not press forward. Instead, they shrunk back into the safety of what they knew.

Gideon climbed out of the hole he was hiding in and stepped into new territories defeating his enemies in the strength and wisdom of God. These days are not over unless we shrink back. Rise, men and women of God. Know that if God is for you, you are victorious. Now, walk it out! Every action, attitude, and agenda be submitted to Him! Go forward, not for yourself, but as a commissioned child of God, and answer to His authority in your life.

Onward! Upward! Outward! *Go*...Live a life of integrity, authentic faith, fearlessness, and courage in the face of all odds, pure and holy in *His* empowerment! Be a Gideon! God dares you!

Launch Out

When He had stopped speaking, He said to Simon, "Launch out into the deep and let down your nets for a catch." But Simon answered and said to Him, "Master, we have toiled all night and caught nothing; nevertheless at Your word I will let down the net."
Luke 5:4-5

When was the last time you heard a call to launch out into the deep?

Can you imagine being Peter—a fisherman all his life, after having fished all night, hauling in massive, empty, dirty nets and then in the midst of cleaning them beachside—hearing Jesus commission him to reload those nets, and hoist the sails, to launch out into the deep water again, midday?

I think if I were Peter, my first argument would be, "You're a carpenter, what do you know about fishing?" My second would be, "I'm too hungry." Yet, Peter (who may have thought those things) obeys Jesus' command. Amazing. His reward of faithfulness? A giant catch.

Are we willing to launch out into the deep? Granted, sometimes it seems too overwhelming to consider the cost, the exertion, and the timing. Our logic gets in the way and says, "This won't work; it's not the right time." Our thoughts can hinder us from the fantastic opportunity, calling it quits just shy of the prize. We expect that if God is going to do something miraculous and overwhelmingly amazing, it will happen in our timing, in ways we understand and can replicate. We don't want to go through the rigors and exertion of "launching out" into deep waters we can't swim in. But that's when the catch will happen.

I have to load the nets, get the sail up, row out, and then trust that what He commissioned, He will accomplish by supplying what I cannot.

He wants us to participate with Him in this incredible journey of faith. It is not just sitting on the shore and waiting for God to bring it all to me, He said, "Launch out," which requires much of me in energy, faith, and obedience.

What about you? Has God called you to launch out into the deep? Has he put something in your heart that you can't do on your own? If He called you to it, He would provide the completion of it.

For Every Doubting Thomas

The other disciples therefore said to him, "We have seen the Lord." So he said to them, "Unless I see in His hands the print of the nails, and put my finger into the print of the nails, and put my hand into His side, I will not believe."
John 20:25

The reactions of the disciples in all of the different scenarios that we see play out in Scripture are genuinely surprising. So often we just glance over them without a second thought. Yet, I love to put myself in the scenario.

How would I have reacted to all of the other disciples telling me they had just seen Jesus alive. Probably something like this, *"Oh Really? It's been three long, terrifying days, where we've been hunted like animals. We've been hiding out together, scurrying around town to replenish food supplies. We're desperately trying to think of a plan to stay safe and wrap our heads around what happened here. The man we gave up everything for and followed the last three years, has been jailed, tried, mocked, beaten and crucified. We gave up all that we owned. We left the comfort of our families and friends, have no place to run or return to, and all our hopes of a messiah have been dashed to pieces. Well unless I can put my hands in his wounds and his side, I won't believe it! How nice that He showed up for you. I want to see him myself. Sorry I am not satisfied with a second-hand account. It is just too unbelievable, and too heartbreaking if it were to turn out to be false. I'll need to see Him myself!"*

Yeah. That's pretty much how I think I would react. Having been heartbroken, with no hope left, I would not want to be lied to with some false comfort. I would rather face the truth head-on and try to move forward than to believe anything secondhand.

I love this story. Why? Many will think it was terrible of Thomas to have doubted. He wanted evidence to prove their words. Yet, I think it was an exciting display of desire! Of course, he wanted Jesus to be alive! Of course, he would have been amazed and thrilled with the idea, but remember that what they all experienced was horrific, traumatic, and devastating. He was not willing to be satisfied with secondhand information. He wanted a personal, one-on-one encounter with Jesus. If Christ were indeed risen from the dead, it wouldn't be any real trouble to grant that encounter.

How bold. How personal. How compelling. How intimate.

Jesus made sure that He took the time to encounter Thomas. Not because Thomas demanded it, but because He is God, righteous and just, and desires personal intimacy with each of His disciples.

I am like Thomas. I don't believe things because they are preached to me. I was raised by both my mother and father to exercise faith while searching things out and testing everything. Now, that doesn't mean I don't end up sometimes feeling like I've been duped. I've had my share of gullible moments. This has caused the resolve in me to rise up all the more.

I love to see this in Thomas. I love the hands-on knowledge he was seeking, the one-on-one, the visual connection, the real understanding he was pleading for to prove against all impossibilities that this was real.

How persistent are you in your pursuit of God? Would you be willing in a crowd of believers to say what Thomas said? Think of how they all gasped when he said what he did. Yet he stood his ground, not to blast them or make them feel bad, or even to disagree with them, but to say that he wanted a personal encounter as well and wouldn't be satisfied with a secondhand account.

Jesus honored his deep heart-wrenching desire by meeting Thomas face to face. At that moment, Thomas proclaimed, "My Lord and My God!" There was no turning back. There would never again be any hesitation. Now, as a fully assured and committed servant, he would forever proclaim Jesus as his Lord and God! That's huge. And that's why Jesus showed up: not to satisfy some fanciful curiosity, not to pander to a wistful begging of a sign, but to anchor and secure an unwavering faith for all future trials. (If you know the way Jesus died, you'll understand why Thomas would need to be fully assured).

God is willing to make Himself understandable to secure our faith. He wants us to stand firm in the midst of all that will come at us in the future. Sometimes this is a one-time impact, other times it is one layer of truth built upon another; brick by brick.

If you have doubts, bring them to God. He wants you to know Him personally, one-on-one. He may display something to you, or He may call you to put your hands in his side, to dig into the Scriptures for the answer—not satisfied by what is told you by others, but personally encountering and intimately seeing the various aspects of who He is, as you dive deeper in His Word.

Dinner is Served

So they saw God, and they ate and drank.
Exodus 24:11

In the book of Exodus, there is a unique encounter that Moses
and the seventy-five elders had with God. He invited them up to
the top of a mountain that was ablaze with fire, smoke, and loud
booming noises. As they climbed the mountain—fearful I'm
sure—they were eventually met with the very presence of God
himself. They saw Him. Well, at least they saw his feet.

"Then Moses went up, also Aaron, Nadab, and Abihu, and
seventy of the elders of Israel, and they saw the God of Israel.
And there was under His feet as it were a paved work of sapphire
stone, and it was like the very heavens in its clarity. But on the
nobles of the children of Israel He did not lay His hand. So they
saw God, and they ate and drank". (Exodus 24:9-11).

This is a fantastic encounter. I wonder if they mention viewing
His feet because they were terrified to look any higher. I bet
they all fell on their faces in sheer terror of what could become of
them seeing God Himself.
I don't know about you, but I would have been trembling in my
shoes like the tin man and lion before the Wizard of Oz. There
was always the understanding that no one could see God and
live.

These seventy-five men saw God. They already heard God. Days earlier, they'd heard the audible voice of God declaring the Ten Commandments to the entire nation. They had seen how God vanquished all the false gods of Egypt with crushing blows as He came against the top ten gods of the land with specific plagues purposed to expose their impotence.

These men knew that if you were to see God, you'd die, and *yet*, they didn't. They, instead, were given food and drink. A banquet was prepared for them. God called them to dinner, to sup with Him, to come and sit for a while and meet with Him, to learn of Him.

Why?

Why do we spend time lavishing on others with good hospitality? To lovingly show that they are valued, precious, and cared for.

God has a unique way of taking care of His people. As powerfully frightening as He can be, He is also tender, loving, and intimately acquainted with our needs. He displayed His mercy, compassion, and desire for fellowship to the elders so they could, in turn, share this truth with their own tribes.

God desires us to know that He can prepare a table for us, to satisfy, comfort, and nourish us. Ultimately, He calls each one of us to answer the call to feast with Him on a mountain that may be somewhat fearful, and yet marvelously prepared.

When was the last time you sat at the table with Him, learned, listened, and surrendered to what was prepared for you as His guest?

He is a God of incredible wonder. He desires a relationship with us. He invites us to come into His territory, an eerily-set-ablaze mountaintop.

Are we willing to endure the climb?
Are we humbled by the intensity of the moment?
Do we leave that place considering it a small thing?
Do we become forgetful of His authority and act rebelliously?

Or

Are we forever changed and transformed having seen the feet of Him who is lovely and full of wonder, of Him who walks on a pavement of sapphire, clear as crystal, of Him whose feet bring good news?

Salt and Light: Taste and See

Oh, taste and see that the Lord is good;
Blessed is the man who trusts in Him!
Psalm 34:8

I love the parallels you find throughout the Scriptures. They fascinate me. How many of us have heard the Scripture, "Taste and see that the Lord is good," and associated it with what Jesus says to us: "You are the salt of the earth, you are the light of the world" (Matthew 5:13-16, paraphrased)?

The comparison is obvious. We are the only tangible thing that the world can experience to help them understand God aside from reading the Scriptures. Our lives, lifestyle, actions are all to reflect an aspect of the Lord. Our lives should be flavored glimpses of Jesus Christ.

That's a tall order. And yes, there are those that have called themselves "Christians" and proved with their actions that they were anything but followers of Jesus Christ!

When I hear the Scripture, "Taste and see," I do not think sweet sugar, dessert, or candy; I think of comfort foods. I love a good juicy steak, chicken soup, or lasagna. I imagine food that would nourish me with minerals and vitamins, things I would never get from sugar. Solid food, sustaining food.

When Jesus calls us the salt of the earth and the light of the world He does so because we are His ambassadors on the planet. If we as ambassadors, as salt, as light, are more concerned with *His* reputation than our own wants and justifications of error, we not only bring more pleasure to Him, but also more blessing on our own heads, and are better witnesses of His Kingdom. We are called to be salt and light in a rotting and desperately darkened world.

Knowing who Jesus is, and what He has done for us, becomes our light—a light that sets our path ablaze, and a light that exposes our sin to our own eyes so that we would repent and turn away from it. A light gives us the warmth and comfort of understanding what is ahead of us, and where we are at in life. If light shines on hurting hearts, then we can see how to extend help. Lighthouses give light to ships at sea, a porch light helps others see where the steps are, and street lights help drivers not feel so afraid on unfamiliar roads. Are we being a light to others? We are called to be light, helping to give a bit of the same light we understand to those who are walking on paths near us.

We are called to be salt, to prevent that which causes rot and decay. A little salt goes a long way. Salt creates thirst. Salt has essential minerals. Pink Himalayan salt has eighty-four trace minerals that are good for your body. But too much salt in foods would ruin it and make it inedible. Ever make a batch of cookies and substitute white salt for sugar, yuck!

As Christians, are our words seasoned with salt, or do we pour the salt on like those disgusting cookies? A little salt on the tongue makes people crave more, like a bag of potato chips, but a tablespoon of salt is too much to swallow. Measure it out wisely when you speak.

"Walk in wisdom toward those who are outside, redeeming the time. Let your speech always be with grace, seasoned with salt, that you may know how you ought to answer each one." (Colossians 4:5-6).

"Let no one deceive you with empty words, for because of these things the wrath of God comes upon the sons of disobedience. Therefore do not be partakers with them. For you were once darkness, but now you are light in the Lord. Walk as children of light (for the fruit of the Spirit is in all goodness, righteousness, and truth), finding out what is acceptable to the Lord. And have no fellowship with the unfruitful works of darkness, but rather expose them. For it is shameful even to speak of those things which are done by them in secret. But all things that are exposed are made manifest by the light, for whatever makes manifest is light." (Ephesians 5:6 -13).

Got Fruit?

The fruit of the righteous is a tree of life, And he who wins souls is wise.
Proverbs 11:30

As a kid, I have some very distinct memories linked to fruit. Since I was very young, I loved Thanksgiving because I was able to eat pomegranates. I remember as a kid picking wild raspberries and blackberries in the woods to make jam, or snacking blueberries that grew on a huge bush in my grandparents' backyard. I also remember picking buckets of fresh strawberries in the spring or making grape jelly from the vines in our backyard. We climbed a large fig tree in Louisiana, picking buckets of tasty figs. My grandfather had a huge apple tree, so large I couldn't climb it to reach them. In the fall, the tree dropped them, all leaving a mess of rotting apples. It was always strange that we were never able to enjoy them.

I also remember walking into someone's dining room and seeing a delicious bowl of fruit, only to find out they were plastic.

Fruit is produced for the benefit of others. Animals and humans enjoy the fruit of trees, vines, and other plants. It can be the sweet fleshy peach, apple, orange, banana, pineapple or even grains, olives and nuts, just to mention a few. It's all fruit, full of unique flavors, vitamins, and various other nutrients ordained by God to sustain us in life, healthy, whole, abundantly.

The fruit of the plant is the edible nutritious portion of the plant, often the flesh around the seed.

I have always told my kids, you need to judge the fruit of individuals. Do they have good fruit, or is it rotten? Will it nourish you or make you sick? Some have asked, "Why judge others fruit?" Well, for one, Jesus told us to in Matthew 7:15-27. The main reason is that judging others' fruit safeguards you. You can't change them, you can't issue a sentence on them for bad fruit, but you can and should safeguard yourself, your family, your future and your investments if you determine the value, worth and ability of someone else's fruit.

Would you eat rotten fruit? No. Why? Because it can make you sick. Did you just judge that fruit? Yes. Was it a malicious judgement against the fruit? No. It was a wise judgement on your behalf. Leave the rotting fruit on the tree or on the ground where it fell, there are other creatures that will benefit from it, not you.

If you can see that someone is faithful, you can trust them to keep their promises. If someone has proven that they are not, you are foolish for believing their word and giving them any responsibility, your heart or your riches. If someone is short-tempered, contentious, angry or argumentative, then they are usually selfish and controlling. If someone is patient and kind, you can receive sweet nutrition from their heart, and be revived when you have a weary soul…get it?

Remember, though, that not all fruit is juicy and sweet. Some have other textures, flavors, and nutritional qualities. So, don't think that for someone to have the fruit of the Spirit, it always has to be sweet and to your liking. Some fruit is dry, hard or seemingly tasteless, but is still good fruit. Olives, coconut, avocados, grains, for instance, are not like the sweet fruit of the grape, fig, peach or watermelon. These are a completely different types of fruit with different qualities.

Fruit is by far more valuable than the gifts of the Spirit. One is temporal, and one is eternal. First Corinthians 13 tells us that pretty plainly. It even goes on to say that gifts will cease, whereas love, a fruit of the Spirit, is forever.

So, are we paying attention to the fruit in our life, or the lack of it? Do we know what the fruit is? What it really looks like? What it isn't? Its opposites are apparent, but the counterfeits— well, now there's those darn pieces of plastic fruit again! Continually ask the Lord to produce in and through you true fruit by His Spirit. This fruit comes from having deep roots in His Word and personal relationship with Him; fruit that is not only nourishing to those around you, but also bearing seeds that will germinate, take root and grow into new plants.

What's your fruit like?

Don't Quit at the Halfway Point!

...And Terah took his son Abram and his grandson Lot, the son of Haran, and his daughter-in-law Sarai, his son Abram's wife, and they went out with them from Ur of the Chaldeans to go to the land of Canaan; and they came to Haran and dwelt there...
Genesis 11:26 - 12:4

Don't stop at the halfway point. This Christian walk can be strenuous. Keeping it pure and staying faithful and true to God is not always easy. Life takes turns, we lose loved ones, and bad things happen and rattle us to the core. Walking the trail is hard. With all the things that come at us—pressures, temptations, selfish wants, pain, sickness, death, betrayals, sorrows, losses— It's all so tricky. But I would encourage you: stay the course. Don't stop at the halfway point, things are going to happen regardless!

Life is hard. Jesus isn't a magic potion or fairy godfather that makes all the boo-boos, aches and pains, go away. He equips, encourages, and engages us as we deal with all of life's issues. If we quit, we lose out!

Look at the end of Genesis 11 and into 12, at the story of the call of Abram and Terah his dad. Terah had sons when he was seventy years old. At some point, his first-born son, Haran, dies. Years after Haran's death, Terah picks up his remaining family members —his son Abram and Haran's son Lot and their wives—to move west to Canaan, to the land God calls promised

He travels with all of them and gets to a certain point and stops, unwilling to go further.

The narrative tells us it is a place called Haran. Is it a coincidence? I doubt it, God always has something to say in His words. Terah "settled" there.

Maybe it was originally a desolate place Terah helped establish and build into a city, or a place he renamed after his son's loss; some sort of shrine to memorialize his son Haran. Maybe it was a town already called Haran. Regardless, he never got past Haran.

Sadly, Haran is about halfway on the journey to the promised land. His other son, Abram, had to pick up the pieces and carry on without his dad and finish what his dad had started. Abram heard the call of God to go to the Promised Land, so he picked up the family and headed out to finish the trek.

What many people that read the story don't realize is, Abram went on to the Promised Land while his dad was still alive.

When you do the math, God called Abram at seventy-five, making Terah only 145, and yet he died in Haran at 205, so he lived sixty years after Abram left to continue to follow the Lord.

What caused Terah to stop following God? Was it the pain, the loss of Haran, his son? Was he unwilling to leave behind and memorial or city development he may have initiated in his son's honor or namesake? All we know is that he didn't move past Haran. You can't tell me it wasn't because of his son's association with the name of that city.

Some ask the question: then why did God mention that Terah died, before we read about the mention of God calling Abram to continue on? Perhaps it was because Terah was no longer willing to be useful for God. He wanted it the way it was; no more challenges, no more sacrifices. Terah found where he wanted to be and was willing to be left there. Stuck in his grief, willing to lose all other family members, not seeing any future, because he tied it all up in one son. Whatever the case, this was his comfort zone, and he wasn't willing to move anymore, not even for God.

This life is not easy, sometimes it is treacherous. It is filled with snags and heartbreak, Christian or not. That said, don't stop moving toward the things God has called you to. Don't get stuck in Haran. Interestingly, his name means, desolate place, barrenness. Getting stuck in the hurts makes us desolate, desperate, depressed and despairing of all hope.

The reward is not far off. Keep moving forward. Don't quit at the halfway point. Be willing to let go of the past hurts. Move forward and receive the prize, in spite of the losses.

Desires Given

Delight yourself also in the Lord,
And He shall give you the desires of your heart.
Psalm 37:4

"Oh, goodie, God! I want this, and that…I want to be happy and frivolous…I want all my wishes to be lavishly set in order before me so that I can bask in the glory of having them all to myself."

Okay, so, none of us actually pray like that, but there are those times we may have gotten close.

The Scripture says, *"Delight yourself in the Lord, and He will give you the desires of your heart."* So, what does this Scripture really mean? Is God going to grant me all the wishes and wants of my heart just because I believe in Him, or I believe He wants me to be happy?

First, do we delight in the Lord? Do we find our pleasure in serving Him? Do we love the things that He loves, and do we abstain or despise the things which He despises? Do we love righteousness, truth, and justice, even when it seemingly corrects us? Are we willing to change our attitudes towards sin we once embraced as acceptable when we find out the Lord is not pleased with them?

Do we enjoy obeying His will? Do we find fulfillment in saying no to the former way of life and living in the newness of the

Spirit? I'm not talking about legalism here; I'm talking about truth. Do we read the Scriptures in light of His Spirit and get convicted of our sin? Do we find ourselves repenting of it and changing our behaviors and ultimately our mindset? Or do we just continue on as we were?

Many times, Christians have become disillusioned with God, angry at God and even going so far as rejecting God. Why? Often because they didn't get what they wanted, because God wouldn't fulfill their personal desires.

I would ask, did you think He was your genie in a bottle? Is God so small that we think we can become His master and make demands of Him?

Where does it say that God is at our command to give us our wish list just because we proclaim Him as our God? Being human and flawed in our understandings, we often look at this Scripture and say, "Oh see, God says that he will give me the 'fulfillment'" of my desires" and when he doesn't, they hold a grudge against Him, as if He was their slave and rebellious to their demands.

But that is not what this Scripture is saying. It is saying that we must delight ourselves in Him. Find all our delight in Him. Focus entirely on Him and no other.

He will then place within us His desires, as seeds that will grow into desires we too will want and yearn for. He will give us the actual desires.

If the desires come from Him, He will either bring them to pass or help us be satisfied in the pursuit of them. Not all those mentioned as pillars of faith in Hebrews 11 received the fulfillment of the promises of God or the "desires" God had given them, yet they pursued Him regardless.

Do we today have the stick-to-it-iveness, tenacity, and a sold-out pursuit of Christ mentality? To delight in Him is to pursue Him, the giver and not the gifts. He is the source of life itself. As we seek Him, our initial desires fade from view, and His desires become our reward...

In the Flesh, God!

In the beginning was the Word, and the Word was with God,
and the Word was God. He was in the beginning with God. 3
All things were made through Him, and without Him nothing
was made that was made. In Him was life, and the life was the
light of men. And the light shines in the darkness, and the
darkness did not comprehend it...And the Word became flesh
and dwelt among us, and we beheld His glory, the glory as of
the only begotten of the Father, full of grace and truth.
John 1:1-14

The thought of God incarnate is not a small thought. Prophets for
millennia could not fully fathom its depths. Commentaries and
countless books have been written about this idea. It is a massive
thought to ponder. Indeed, I'm not going to cover it but a grain of
sand's worth here.

To think that God would give up anything to become a human is
beyond me. It is hard to imagine God concealing Himself in a
small human form. It stretches the mind trying to grasp the
limitations He would willingly subject Himself to just so He
could be acquainted with our griefs and our sorrows. It is more
than I can seem to understand from my small, finite and selfish
perspective.

In my human frame, I look at it all and realize, I would not do the
same. I do not do the same.

How often I am led by my own selfish motivations, unwilling to go to lengths of such significance. It is not in mankind's ability or power. There is no resource within us to be able to accomplish the same measure of self-sacrifice. For one, we are only fully human, born under the curse of sin, and therefore, sinful. Jesus was fully human, but he was also entirely *God*! There's the game changer!

Why is Christmas so wonderful? Is it so that we can "Ooh" and "Ahh" over Jesus, the sweet little baby in the manger? Could it be deeper? Think of the angels that heralded the news to the shepherds in the field that night. They were amazed. They were stunned at the enormity of it. They shouted and exclaimed, amazed that God, the One who spoke all things into existence, would limit Himself and embed Himself into a world so torn, broken, and destitute. Why would God submit Himself to a sinful, hate filled and rebellious creation? His love for a creation made in His image drove Him to pay the price for our sin. To give us opportunity to be reconciled to Him again, He needed a perfect Human to pay the toll for sin. For that, He had to take on the form of humanity

Oh, my God! Why would you do such a thing for me? How is it that You didn't think this unfitting for You to do? Why would You enter my world to Humble yourself, giving up your throne for a feeding troth?

No wonder the angels heralded His coming. They knew He was worthy! No wonder they looked on, perplexed and amazed at the greatest gift to man, that He would come, compelled by love, to restore a creation that was completely lost and without hope had He not come!

I pray that each person gets to enjoy the season of love, peace, and joy. The love of God that compelled Him to incarnate human flesh, to be acquainted with our griefs and sorrows, living among us, dying for us and rising in power to prove His ability to restore us. Such love brings a rejoining, redeeming and reconciling. This is true peace, and that understanding anchors our hearts in the most tumultuous of situations, assuring our hearts and strengthening our souls with pure joy.

I don't think we are to live as if today is to be our last and try to set all of our ducks in a row before we meet our maker. But to *live* as if it is our first, out of amazement, awe, and a security and power stronger than death. This revelation helps us see eternity, and His throne as more real, more tangible, more substantial than any earthly happiness or trial.

May we each allow the truths of each season, regardless of when in the year it is, to awaken our desperate hearts.

Redefined by God, Not Garbage

Brethren, I do not count myself to have apprehended; but one thing I do, forgetting those things which are behind and reaching forward to those things which are ahead, I press toward the goal for the prize of the upward call of God in Christ Jesus.
Philippians 3:13-14

How many of us struggle with our identity?
Ezekiel 16 describes a woman that has grown up in a rather unusual environment: in her own blood!
How many of us have made some pretty bad choices in life somewhere along the way, Christian or not? How many of us continued in the shame and guilt of those choices?

Often, I refer back to this Scripture in Ezekiel because, starting in verse 6, here is a young woman that the Lord has taken notice of who is wallowing in her own blood! She has grown up in it. What a horrible past this young lady has: despised, rejected, neglected unloved and *yet* God's tender mercy takes her, covers her, swears Himself to her, cleans her, washes her, places beautiful ornaments of His splendor and glory on Her, and raises her up to a position of royalty!

A true rags-to-riches love story! Unfortunately, she gets a bit prideful and boastful as if she has secured these things in herself and she falls away from the one that loved, redeemed, and glorified her. Eventually, she is restored, not because of her goodness but because of *His*!

I love sharing this message of hope and restoration! I often get together with women who need this kind of encouragement.

Matthew 1 shows four fantastic displays of mercy. There were four women mentioned in the Lineage of Jesus Christ: Tamar, Rahab, Ruth, and Bathsheba. All four women had soiled pasts! Yet, God in his love for them, and their willingness to submit and walk in faith, brought them into a place of receiving God's abundant love for them. Tamar was refused, neglected and uncared for by her family members; Rahab was a prostitute and a pagan; Ruth was a descendant of Moab, which was a tribe started in incest and considered an enemy of God's people; and Bathsheba was raped, her husband killed, and her child died. Yet God intervened in their lives and reset their course to *His* coordinates! They found hope and life in the God of Israel. They could have stayed where they were remaining in despair, but instead, they chose God and His life, regardless of the cost!

In doing so, He redefined who they were and what fruit they would bring forth in their lives. If they had allowed their past, their families history to define them, they never would have been changed! Instead, they believed the promises of God, not just in mental ascent, but in their day-to-day walk—in their submission to His kingdom, and His authority for their lives.

He, in turn, made them new, fully embracing and accepting them into the promises that He pours out on those who obey Him.

Philippians 3:14 says that we are to forget those things which lie behind us and press forward into the high call of God which is found in Christ Jesus

Remember what 2 Corinthians 2:17 says— that if *anyone* is found *in* Christ, [S]he is a new creation; all things have passed away. Behold, all things become new!

I pray you will all find yourselves hidden in Him. Unless we dwell in His presence, we will never find out who we are.

Like Getting Water from a Rock!

And they did not thirst When He led them through the deserts;
He caused the waters to flow from the rock for them;
He also split the rock, and the waters gushed out.
Isaiah 48:21

Can't get water from a rock, right? *Wrong!* Well spiritually speaking, anyway!

In the book of Exodus, the children of Israel find themselves walking through the wilderness. Parched and thirsty, they rushed Moses and clamored for water. They were threatening his very life, ready to stone him (Ex 17:1-7).

How many times in my life have I run to the Lord, my Rock, and my Redeemer in a panic or overcome with anxiety for various reasons, hurting, hungry, thirsty? I've run to God complaining, pleading, desperate, in fear or agony, demanding He do something.

In my clamoring, I've been guilty of knocking others down, threatening and willing to take matters into my own hands. Thankfully, the Lord rebuked and corrected me. I found His rebukes to be a comfort when I was willing to receive them. If I seek Him in desperate times, knowing He is my only source of strength, my rock, He will command His water to flow and refresh me. He will give a renewed strength in that moment. Similar to when Hagar, Abraham's concubine, was told to leave with her teenage son, and found herself without water in the middle of the desert. Just when she thought it was over and they would perish, an angel of the Lord reveals a water source for her and her son, and promised a future, giving her hope (Gen. 21:14-20).

Then as Moses needed to do that another time, thirty-eight later, the people were without water once again. Again, they clamored against Moses, threatening to kill him. After he cried out, God told him this time to speak to the rock, and it would give water (Num 20:3-13). He was so frustrated with the situation, he struck the rock, not just once, but twice.

Even after many years on the journey with the Lord, having grown and learned so much, yet there are times when the situations around me, overwhelm and frustrate me. I find myself striking out at the rock to procure the water I'm desperate for once again.

Anyone ever been there?

Has anyone ever gotten so crazed by life that they rush on Jesus in full panic? Well, I've been there and done that. I will probably do it again (though I'd like to say I wouldn't, I'm weak). But God is good! Even though we panic from time to time, even among the mature in Christ, God is faithful to present Himself strong!

In the panic of the waves, Jesus rose up and rebuked the wind and then his disciples, but didn't give up on them.

In the frustration of striking the rock, God still supplied the water and then dealt with Moses personally.

God is still good, even in our moments of being exacerbated.

Two Trees

And out of the ground the LORD God made every tree grow that is pleasant to the sight and good for food. The tree of life was also in the midst of the garden, and the tree of the knowledge of good and evil.
Genesis 2:9

In the first few chapters of Genesis, there's an account of the two trees in the Garden of Eden. One tree's fruit offers life, and the other tree's fruit provides the knowledge of good and evil.

I have been asked often several questions about these trees. What were they? Was one of the trees an apple? Was the second tree deadly? Why would God put the second tree there if it was going to cause them to die? Why would a good God put in a bad tree? Why would He tell them not to eat it and then put it there? Why would God test them like that?

I believe God is good! And everything He makes has the ability to produce good in our lives. I don't think the tree of the knowledge of good and evil was terrible, evil, wrong, a mistake, a malicious temptation, a trick, or deadly.

I stress to my kids all the time: some things come with age, maturity, responsibility, proven track records., etc. I personally believe it was the same thing with that tree...I think there was a restriction on it, for that time, season, duration and in the beginning. after they matured, faithfully executed their given responsibilities and continued learning from Him, God may have eventually given them the "ok" to eat from it, when they could handle it wisely.

I wouldn't give my fourteen-year-old the car keys, because some things come with age and maturity, and have predetermined boundaries to keep everyone safe. But see, that's the key: It's waiting and trusting God that *He knows* when things are best to be in our lives, not grasping for it ahead of time.

Someone asked me if the tree represented sin...the answer is *no*! It represents anything that has a marked boundary, within the confines of God's timing, place, and approval. Knowing good and evil is not sin, but grasping and engaging in the experience of something God has currently said is off limits to us, and therefore outside the blessing of God at this time, is sin. With sex as an example, sex is not bad. Sex was created by God, for pleasure, purpose, and promise. It is to be thoroughly enjoyed within the confines of the boundaries He has set. Outside of that umbrella, there is a problem, a consequence, and an error, and thereby sinful, not receiving His blessing.

Even ministry that we are called to, if we are seeking it instead of God, we have then pursued grasping a fruit outside the timing and approval of God. That fruit has become an idol, and Satan then has open ground and a prepared heart to deceive. The Bible is pretty clear: we are drawn away from God by our own lust. Satan baits us, then plays with us, saying, "has God said you should not do this or that, be this or that, pursue this or that, enjoy this or that, have this or that" He puts the very thing that

God may eventually want us to partake of in the future, before our face, has us examine it with our intellect, see that it is pleasurable to the eye and good for food to make one wise, and then has us question God's timing, purpose, and goodness. *Don't fall for it!*

The Bible makes it clear in Hebrews that Moses knew he was to deliver the children of Israel while living in the palace of Egypt. He acted on it in his own timing—his own understanding—and killed an Egyptian taskmaster. He ran ahead of God's plan, grasping at something he knew was his calling before God had told him to deliver them. He ended up on the run for the next forty years.

This is when we have to seek God out, allow Him to be on the throne of our heart, and trust that His timing, His truth, and His will for our lives are abundant towards us. Then, we can resist the devil's taunting and repent of our own pride/lust and idolatry of that thing.

Overall, this tree is something we willingly partake of anytime we desire something due to our selfish pride, arrogance, and idolatry of self. We want to be on the throne of our own heart, and we assume we have the ability, strength, maturity, and right to that which we desire.

Satan is not the culprit; he merely gives voice to something we already have in our heart, and gives an opportunity for us to justify our own error. Eve was not the only one who dealt with this, folks. We all do. No one is exempt from this. Consider the things you clamor for, the things that disappoint you and cause you to get frustrated or angry when you don't have them in your way and in your time.

Remember, our hearts are deceitful. We are very good at deceiving ourselves and justifying with "good intentions" our idolatrous hearts and grabbing for fruit we shouldn't be eating.

Surrender it all to Christ again, taking every thought captive to Him. This is our only hope of walking in His will!

God Keeps What Has Been Entrusted to Him

For this reason I also suffer these things; nevertheless I am not ashamed, for I know whom I have believed and am persuaded that He is able to keep what I have committed to Him until that Day.
2 Timothy 1:12

It's incredible how beautiful having children is. I don't know about you, but I go in cycles praying for my children. Sometimes, it is pretty routine, while other times it is intense, depending on circumstances, my own shortcomings or choices they have made.

My children are grown. I miss the simpler times and simple problems. The other part of me is enjoying watching them step into their own lives and branch out and learn what it means to be an adult.

My kids have had their bouts with pain, frustration and hurt over the years. They've seen dear friends die, been in car accidents, dealt with intense life choices and suffered some very deep betrayals. Yet they continue to stride forward, stronger as a result.

With all of my children, I have come to understand that though my carnal mind and soul might want to do everything for them, keep them in a bubble, isolate them, and hover over them, I can't. I should neither harshly punish bad behavior, hoping to scare them away from those choices, nor enable and justify their actions.

To react either of those ways for me would be entirely based out of fear and lack of trusting God.

In a sense, I would be idolizing them. Instead, I need to place and entrust God with their lives— the good, bad and ugly, the blessings and the consequences. I need to be confident that God has this! Even when they make terrible choices, those choices have implications I cannot remove. I need to believe that even the judgments of God are executed in perfection and for one purpose: to be merciful. A rebuke or consequence is a mild spanking that puts us check and causes us to back away from things that would utterly destroy us. Discipline is the mercy of God, even if we are not willing to see it.

I decided a while ago not to allow—that's right, allow, give permission, surrender myself to, become a slave of—the "fear" of my children being hurt, spiritual, mentally, and physically (in that order). I have done what I know to do and will continue to do so, keeping my boundaries, my prayers, and my influence in their lives, where I know God wants them to be. I must believe He has the power to keep safe what has been entrusted to him.

As I remain faithful, my parental weaknesses are covered in His grace. God will prove Himself when the time is right, and I will rejoice in the knowledge that God has kept my children according to His own purpose and their willingness, regardless of what my kids go through, face, endure, or are challenged or hurt by.

He kept me, so He can keep them.

Oh, You Make Me So Mad!

"Be angry, and do not sin": do not let the sun go down
on your wrath,
Ephesians 4:26

Ever get so mad that you just can't control yourself? Ever get so frustrated by things that you act out, perhaps even violently?

Years ago, I struggled with anger. From time to time, it still rears its ugly head. It took some time to realize why and when I got angry and allowed it to have its way with me. When, you might ask? I got so frustrated with the inability to control someone or something else, when I felt I had an inherent right to getting my way!

Where did that inherent right I thought I had come from?

Well, back in the Garden—yes, that Garden, the first garden—Eden. Satan tempted Eve with something that she was not permitted to have. He twisted her understanding of the boundaries and rules (she wasn't allowed to eat, but God didn't say touching was a problem). Satan twisted her reasoning and assured her that if it seemed pleasing to her eye, it must be good for food. He taunted her with a rationalization that it's within her domain, her right, and being withheld unrighteously, that she must have been serving a lousy god!
Once she took, Adam soon followed. Once confronted with the transgression, Adam immediately burst with blame that tore a

massive rift between all parties, between Adam and God and between Adam and Eve. He said, "the woman that *You* gave me!" Adam scolded and blamed everyone else but himself for his selfish quest for godhood!

Gee, is that where anger comes from: not getting my way? We often are so selfish, demanding all others to bow, to be our own god. That rebellious heart shows itself most arrogantly when we are caught in a willful transgression and have to give account for it, and we become very defensive.

Now, I'm not talking about when we are angered with injustice—impropriety—or unrighteousness. I'm talking about the anger that causes us to sin, Self-Worship (Self Idolatry)! The wrong attitude that says we have the right to what we want. We refuse to answer to anyone for our actions, we have such rebellious hearts. We assume we can have whatever we desire at the expense of others because we are the center of our own universe!

The anger and violence come when we hit a wall, when we've been denied that which we expect to be given or fought back on what we tried to take. Every selfish, egotistical cell in our body and mind cries against the denial of our demands and the reality that we are *not* the center of the universe!

We struggle and fight for things we have no right to control, assuming we can secure them in our own flesh and power of mind or strength. How frail we are, and we don't even realize it. How quickly the idol can be cast down and broken into pieces!

Self-control, the control of self, is a fruit of the Spirit. It is contrary to our sinful, selfish nature. Control over self is really the only control we are granted in this life. Yet, we grab for control in so many areas. Real self-control is worked in us, by the Holy Spirit's power. Restraint is not achieved by self-deprivation; it is worked in us when we let the Holy Spirit discipline and correct us. It is only achieved by the Holy Spirit's powerful work changing our flawed and fallen understandings and debunking the myths of the Garden.

> We are not gods.
> We cannot be gods.

There is only *one* God, and He will not give His glory to another. The sooner we surrender to that understanding, the more anchored we are in Him and the less frustrated we are with life's inevitable kinks.

I Can't Do That, God!

But be doers of the word, and not hearers only,
deceiving yourselves.
James 1:22

A few years ago, my neighbor was pregnant with her first child. It was a difficult pregnancy, as she was bedridden within the early weeks. I would go over and break up the monotony and end by praying for her, laying my hands on her and asking the Lord for safe keeping of this precious child.

I knew she liked to read, so when I saw a catalog of books from a Christian book club, I decided to purchase several through the mail to help her pass the next six months. I spent time trying to determine which ones would be best. I prayed for the Lord's wisdom and help. She liked country things, and she is very much a crafty homemaker. I also wanted something that would speak of the love Jesus had for her, since she was not a believer. As I was flipping through the pages, I was suddenly struck by a cover with two little hands, that were from a newborn premature baby.

When I say struck—I mean struck! —I felt like these two little hands leaped off the cover and hit me square in the chest pushing me back in my chair. I started to cry. The name of the book was "*Zoe*," which I knew in Greek meant, "life." I was shocked. The Lord was so loud and specific as He answered my prayer. I knew He was declaring I needed to buy this book and give it to her.

But I couldn't! I had been praying that God would bring this child to gestation. I was speaking in faith that the pregnancy would go to full term. I wouldn't dare give her a book that talked about a preemie. That would scare her, and that would not be in line with the "faith" I was praying over her. It would not be what she wanted, the doctors wanted, or what the baby could deal with at this young age of only 20 weeks.

I couldn't do what I heard God telling me to do.

Instead, I ordered several books, based on her personality. I got her a few that would witness boldly, and one in particular I knew she would like because of the country quilt on the cover and home crafting theme within it. The order form went in and I waited.

I justified my purchase of books, and said that if the Lord wanted her to know, He would tell her Himself. I figured it would be fine if I didn't say it.

I deceived myself.

It was before the days of Amazon Prime and two-day shipping. The purchase took about four weeks to be processed and delivered. I actually forgot about it as the weeks passed.

One day, four weeks later, I got a call from my neighbor's husband. She had gone into early labor. There were some complications, so they were rushing her to the hospital that morning. He asked me to pray.

I prayed all morning, asking the Lord to speak life to that child, to keep and spare this life, to forgive me for being so selfish and keep what was entrusted to Him. It was scary. It was humbling. It was a prayer of remorse as much as it was a prayer of help for them.

Several hours went by, and there was a knock at the door. I answered it, assuming it would be the husband with news. It was the UPS driver with a delivery. I was so distracted by the day's event that I couldn't fathom what might be inside. I set it down, got a knife, and cut through the tape. As I lifted the flap to see what this was, I gasped as I was smacked up against the wall again by the same two little hands from the catalogue.

Zoe had arrived. I broke down and cried.

How could this be? I know that I did not order it. I refused to do so. I was adamant that I would not give such a message. I would not say what I knew the Lord had told me to say. I checked the receipt and the book *Zoe* was *not* listed. The quilt book was listed, but was *not* inside the box.

God made sure the word would get to her in spite of me. I was humbled and so very thankful that the Lord wouldn't allow me to short change her. From that point on, I prayed for the baby's premature birth and many of the usual complications.

A week or two later, the baby was born. At twenty-four weeks, she was the youngest preemie the hospital's NICU unit had ever dealt with. She was all of 1 ½ pounds and she fit in her father's right hand.

When my neighbor came home from the hospital, I went over with two gifts, one from me and a second gift specially delivered from God, in two separate gift bags. God's gift came with a description similar to what is related here, along with the receipt to show the evidence.

That little precious girl is in perfect health, growing and maturing normally. None of the shortfalls and medical concerns doctors have for preemies were a problem for her.

The family has since moved away, with two more beautiful children, I don't know what the final outcome of their story is, but it doesn't matter. God does!

We need to hear and then act according to His Word, not ours.

What is it that causes us to shrink back, refusing to do what we hear God say? For me, it was my religious pride, fear of failure, fear of instilling fear and of not giving "good" news, and fear of not being liked.

I thank God that He did what He wanted to do, in spite of my rebellion to a direct word. I also am thankful that He still allowed me to be part of the process to teach me a valuable lesson in trusting Him, obeying Him, and being forgiven by Him.

I am grateful that He is faithful to His Word!

"So shall My word be that goes forth from My mouth; It shall not return to Me void, But it shall accomplish what I please, And it shall prosper in the thing for which I sent it" (Isaiah 55:11).

Coins & Pearls

"Again, the kingdom of heaven is like treasure hidden in a field, which a man found and hid; and for joy over it he goes and sells all that he has and buys that field. "Again, the kingdom of heaven is like a merchant seeking beautiful pearls, who, when he had found one pearl of great price, went and sold all that he had and bought it."
Matthew 13:44-46

In July 2010, a man found a pot of silver coins in an open field in England beneath the surface: 52,000 thousand antique coins were found that were dated back to third-century Rome. In July 2012, a man found a pot of gold in Israel: 108 gold coins dating to the Crusades.

Can you imagine the delight, the joy, the explosive excitement they must have had? Such great treasure! For so long it was buried beneath the soil, only recently to have been excavated, redeemed and given new value and appreciation!

Jesus is the man in the parable above that has recognized the huge prize buried in the dirt. He relinquished all that he had to redeem and restore it to a place of predetermined value. No longer hidden, but brought up from the depths to be used for the benefit it was initially intended to have. He was willing to pay whatever price was necessary…and He did.

He gave *His life* to restore us. Each one of us a coin of value, minted with a purpose to be used, to gain and bring increase to the Kingdom of God.

"Let this mind be in you which was also in Christ Jesus, who, being in the form of God, did not consider it robbery to be equal with God, but made Himself of no reputation, taking the form of a bondservant, and coming in the likeness of men. And being found in appearance as a man, He humbled Himself and became obedient to the point of death, even the death of the cross. Therefore God also has highly exalted Him and given Him the name which is above every name" (Philippians 2:5-9).

The "pearl of great price" is also a picture of the value Jesus places on each one of us. Mankind, made in the image of God, has God to spend Himself on us. This was the only way to redeem us back to what He originally purposed.

Pearls are fabulous, and before the cultured pearl explosion, good pearls were more valuable than gold because of their rarity. Only those of power and prestige owned any. The best pearls were reserved exclusively for royalty. Crowns are adorned with them, garments and rings necklaces and earrings only for the most elite.

Jesus goes to great lengths to retrieve us from the dirt of the world and restore us to be a useable commodity in His Kingdom.

There is a River that Flows

Then he brought me back to the door of the temple; and there was water, flowing from under the threshold of the temple toward the east, for the front of the temple faced east; the water was flowing from under the right side of the temple, south of the altar.
Ezekiel 47:1

I wrote the song, "There is a River that Flows," based on this Scripture. I love how rivers cut through territories, divide lands, create gorgeous scenery, and bring life to areas creating banks of lush vegetation.

There is so much wonder, tranquility, power, and beauty in rivers, from their fast and furious rapids and falls, to their docile and deep glass like waters.

This Scripture in Ezekiel is speaking of living water flowing from the threshold of the temple eastward, down mountain ravines and eventually flowing into the Dead Sea. Currently, the Dead Sea has no life in it now because the salt content is far too high for fish. Yet, a day is coming when waters will flow from the threshold of God and bring life to that Dead Sea, and there will be a significant impact due to that flow.

That day will change the Dead Sea to a sea teeming with life! That is miraculous, that is radical, that is mind-blowing! It is interesting to note that this river will impact not just the waters, but the landscape, the commerce, and the communities. A scene destitute of vegetation, barren, lifeless, harsh, and barely inhabited will be a place where trees will line the banks, fruit will be for food and healing, a tremendous variety of fish will be caught with nets, commerce will increase, habitation will take hold, people will flourish, communities will thrive all because Living Water impacted the area.

This is what God wants to do in each one of us. He wants His Living Water to flow into our dead places, our lifeless, barren, uninhabitable places. He wants to change the landscape, make new the environment, produces fruit, provide sustenance, and give purpose and hope for a life well lived.

Jesus alone offers such an incredible transformation. Jesus alone! Yes, it is exclusive to Him! It comes from the threshold of God. It flows out from Him to us.

This river does not show up on a map, *yet*! The Bible tells us when the river will impact the Dead Sea. Zechariah 14 tells us that at the Lord's return, a river will flow from Jerusalem, to the Eastern Sea.

The major river that currently flows to the Dead Sea is the Jordan River, which is always symbolic of death. Crossing the Jordan is symbolic of leaving the old sinful life and entering the Promised Land, as is being baptized in it. Interestingly, in the book of Joshua, the Jordan River, which flows to the Dead Sea, is how the Israelites crossed into the Promised Land. It was miraculously dried up, and the waters were stopped up as far back as to the City of Adam, as soon as the priests' feet carrying the Ark of the Covenant touched the river.

It is the power and Presence of God when it intersects with that which flows from us (Adam), and it stops the flow which is leading down to the Dead Sea in our life. Only Jesus, only God's presence, does such a thing. Not religious thought, not religious activities, or obligations, only the presence of God stops the flow that leads to a dead result, changing it radically, and bringing life to everything it now touches. It's radical! It's hope!

Jesus promised, *"He who believes in Me, as the Scripture has said, out of his heart will flow rivers of living water'"* (John 7:38).

It's the same river mentioned in Revelation 22:1, *"And he showed me a pure river of water of life, clear as crystal, proceeding from the throne of God and of the Lamb."*

There is a river that flows from the threshold of *God*!

I want it flowing in me!

The "Profit" Margin

Or do you not know that your body is the temple of the Holy Spirit who is in you, whom you have from God, and you are not your own? For you were bought at a price; therefore glorify God in your body and in your spirit, which are God's.
1 Corinthians 6:19-20

There are a few television shows I just love. My favorite right now is CNBC's Show, *The Profit* with Marcus Lemonis. I am always amazed to see this show. As an administrative person, it's exciting, and as a Christian, it's piercing!

The show is about business owners who are in desperate need, unable in their own power, strength, and resources to pay their debt, unable to see clearly, dig themselves out of their bad choices, and have asked for help. Many owners, desperate, seek to restore purpose and reenergize the business which has been teetering on the brink of destruction.

If Marcus likes the product, process or people, he invests a significant amount of money and direction to reset the business course. During the show, many bad decisions become obvious and need to be addressed. They are brought forward into the light of a keen eye and corrected. Without some intervention, the trajectory of their business would bring them to foreclosure, bankruptcy or worse. It's not just in trouble; it's failing completely.

People cry out for help knowing they need it, that they cannot survive without someone to help them. They want more than a handout because none of them are looking to close the doors. They hope to be debt-free and strengthen what they've built. The hope is to have someone come in, help them manage it. They don't want to just make ends meet; they want to infuse their businesses with strength and change so that they can thrive beyond any previous expectations.

In steps Marcus. He sees value in the people, process and or product, and offers to pay off their debt and restructure their everyday choices. He gives new hope, new vision, new opportunities, new strength, and new resources, and he proves himself to be someone with the integrity, know-how and personal ability to back up every offer.

Willingly, he puts down a huge check. In exchange, he is 100% in charge. A lot of people want to take the deal. Looking at their desperate situation, though they may be hesitant to give up their control, they see the dead-end and bridge-out sign quickly come upon them. They know they cannot apply the brakes themselves. They know this is their only option for the salvation of all they love.

The hands shake.

Soon after as things start to be changed, the familiar holds them back from moving forward. Marcus demands change to bring back life to the business, but many will fight against the changes. Changes in physical space, processes, and production test their resolve. Changes that create the largest friction are changes in the heart and mind. Relinquishing control is very difficult.

Submitting to someone else's authority is difficult. It would almost be easier just to let him have it and walk away. Some have. Once people realize that their business was bought with a price and they now have to give control to someone else to make it work, they don't like the terms of the agreement. But they weren't the ones who had any authority to set the conditions; they either agreed and took it or said no and walked away. The terms are generous and will create profits for Marcus as well as the original owners. But things *must* change, and all decisions now go through him. They have to give an accurate account of their practices. Hidden agendas, get exposed, bad attitudes are put in check, and accountability is unavoidable. It's a lot more than just taking someone's money, making a better product, or moving some furniture around.

For those that submit to Marcus, they get great satisfaction. They learn and gain understanding, and are able to receive the great reward of diligence, humility and partnering with someone, tough as it is, that is greater than they are.

When I see a show where people work through even humbling moments, I want to rejoice with those business owners. When I look at a business owner selfishly default against such generosity toward them, I am disappointed, upset, even angry that they couldn't see beyond themselves, beyond their selfishness, or beyond their ego.

Spiritual salvation and transformation are just like this. We need to realize where our lives were before we came to Christ. How precious a price He paid for us and how that is supposed to impact us daily! Jesus paid the price for our soul because He values the person, the process and the product. He did it for His pleasure, to bring Him glory, and to bring increase to His Kingdom, not so that we could be debt-free and run back to our old ways.

In oriental cultures, it is traditional that if someone saved your life, your life is now theirs. You surrender to them as a servant, knowing that you would be dead if not for them.

Do we live like that? Do we truly realize how high a price was paid for us, and for what purpose? Is salvation just so we don't go to hell? Is it just so we can say we are His but live completely unaccountable in attitude, actions, and agendas?

I don't think that would go over too well with Marcus. He's walked out of several deals, taken losses, and denied those who would not submit.

Read the second half of Matthew 7, verse 15-29 to see how Jesus feels about those who would not submit.

Don't mistake the goodness of God and the love of God for a pass on obedience to His authority.

Being Yoked to God

Take My yoke upon you and learn from Me, for I am gentle
and lowly in heart, and you will find rest for your souls.
Matthew 11:29

"What does it mean to be yoked to God or yoked by the Spirit?"
I'm not talking about egg yolks. I'm talking about the yoke that
goes around an animal's neck that harnesses it to a plow or cart.
The picture I want you to get in your head is a double yoke,
meaning two oxen or horses are pulling something side by side.

Jesus told us that if we were laden down with heavy burdens, He
would give us rest. He stated that we are to take His yoke upon
us because it is easier and lighter than what we take on in this
world. This Scripture is almost always used when trying to
encourage the weary. The portion that says to take His yoke is
somehow neglected. We assume God doesn't want to burden us
at all. Jesus is, in fact, telling us we are to take on a constraining
yoke and a burden, His!

God rebuked the people of Judah during the time of the prophet
Jeremiah for having broken the yoke and bursting off the bonds
of His leading. For that, He spoke words of desolation against
them.

"What is the yoke for? What purpose is there in being placed
under a burden? Aren't we to be set free? Haven't we received
liberty in Christ?" Yes, and no! A yoke is as much a part of our

freedom and liberty as our salvation. The yoke is for our training process. Training is the breaking of the self-will, reprogramming a formerly wild and unruly animal for the work of service in a new environment, so that one can live in an orderly fashion in the protection and blessing of a master. All of the disciples, except Judas Iscariot, underwent this process and took this yoke on themselves.

James and John were quick to react with violence before they experienced it. They were called Sons of Thunder for wanting to destroy and call down fire on others. Peter was an arrogant, prideful man before he submitted to the yoke.

Paul was undoubtedly yoked by the Lord and sensitive to that yoke after he was literally knocked off his high horse. He recognized when it was steering him to the right or to the left. Paul oftentimes speaks of chains, but never with a sad heart. He understood the purpose of the Holy Spirit in those chains. Though many were physical chains, he recognized the spiritual yoke or chains on him in obedience to God. He saw himself as a slave of Christ.

He encourages in the book of Romans that we should see ourselves as slaves of Christ. We ought to submit to the leading of the Spirit and present our bodies as slaves of righteousness for holiness. It's in doing so that we will have the fruit of that holiness worked out in our lives and, in the end, have everlasting life. He states that those who are led by the Spirit of God, those are the sons of God.

If we are sons of the Father, aren't there rules of the house we should obey? Doesn't every home have some laws, some rules to adhere to? The book of Proverbs mentions these laws and many times equates them with the wisdom of God. We are told not to forsake them, and though they will be graceful ornaments on our head, they will also be chains around our neck. The blessings they grant are long life, prosperity, and the favor of man and God. We are encouraged by the Word of God that if we submit to the leading of the Spirit and willingly obey, we shall have blessings of eternal value.

Being yoked by the Spirit allows us to learn of his ways and go according to His guidance, recognizing His prodding. Bearing the yoke of the Lord and being harnessed by His Spirit strengthens our walk. Due to the resistance involved in carrying the weight of the yoke, our spiritual muscles are increased. The longer we couple ourselves to the Lord, the more mature we become, able to understand what the Lord intends for us.

Staying in the harness, we go further than merely taking on the form of godliness, we become holy. It equips us for tasks beyond our abilities!

I've been in various situations where I was not capable of performing to speed, and yet God used the situation to form me, and because I was willing to come under His harness, He equipped me for it. If we are ready to be yoked by God, willing to go to the fields He sends us to, then we will be increased and strengthened to become the strong laborers He needs and desires!

Being in the yoke with Christ is when we can say, "Where you lead, I will follow," "Your strength (grace) is made strong in my weakness."

Being yoked is being submitted to His authority in our lives and following Him unconditionally.

Trees of Righteousness

The righteous shall flourish like a palm tree,
He shall grow like a cedar in Lebanon.
Psalm 92:12

Ahhhh! Palm trees! That makes it all better! I just love palm trees. They are beautiful to the eye. They shoot up from the ground in the warm climates, out of a sandy base and pierce the blue sky with their gorgeous green palms. So tall, so straight, so majestic.

They truly are amazing. So much so that God in Scripture likens the believer to the palm tree. There are actually several types of palm trees that the believer is likened to. Each one has uniquely different aspects that compare. The date palm tree is unlike the coconut palm that we are often so familiar with here. The date palm tree is not just beautiful; it is considered a resource.

Years before the Gregorian calendar was in effect, the Phoenicians and most cultures went by a 360-day calendar rather than a 365-day calendar. Interestingly, the date palm tree was so admired that the Phoenicians came up with a list of 360 different uses for the tree, one for each day of their calendar year.
The trees were not just a staple food, rich with nutrients, natural sugars, and oils, but the actual tree was used for many purposes—building supplies, roofing, mats, bedding, ropes, and also for medicinal ointments, elixirs, drinks, wine, oil, etc.

In comparison, the believer in Jesus is useful in the Kingdom of God each day. There are many things that we can put our hands to, ways in which we can be a blessing, serve, honor and give to others, enriching their walk and lives for Christ. Consider your effectiveness in the Kingdom of God. Are you making yourself available to the Body of Christ? Are you willing to serve the greater vision of His Kingdom? Do you realize that the fruit you produce is for the effectual working and benefit of others?

How can you be a blessing to the Body of Christ today?

Different Gospels

...forgetting those things which are behind and reaching forward to those things which are ahead, I press toward the goal for the prize of the upward call of God in Christ Jesus. Philippians 3:13b-14

There are different gospels out there. Here are two that are contrary to each other: the gospel of brokenness and the gospel of victory. Essentially, sharing a message that either enables sin or encourages righteousness.

One has *no* impact or life in it...

One gives us permission to stay where we are with the assumption that we won't have to change and can't. That the day-to-day existence is ok with God, that our broken, sinful and flawed person is not just loved by God, but is in fact, our continued expected state of salvation. This gospel preaches it's ok where we are, and not to expect a change in our personal actions, attitudes or agendas. They use statements such as, "God loves you the way you are" as if to say, God embraces our sin, our problems, and is ok with us staying that way (in other words, He condones or sanctions sin as acceptable).

All this does is enable sin to continue. It seems to give the idea that God can't change our heart, nor would He dare to challenge us to live differently. Further, that He expects we will live continually bound by sin, anxieties, desires, thoughts, and emotions which are contrary to His nature and purposes in our life.

Many will use statements like, "God is acquainted with your suffering" as if to say, "God gets it, it's ok." Such statements end up conveying a bad message. Either our lifestyle and sins don't matter to God, or He's unable to help and deliver us.

Others may say such things like "you will probably never be healed, or set free from things like i.e., depression, rage, fear, anxiety, various sins. In their attempt to ease our pain, they are unknowingly saying, "learn to live with the leash the devil controls you with." This is more of an enabling gospel than a true doctrine. It affirms us, our feelings and desires, giving a false sense of acceptance, while allowing our sins, our error, and bad attitudes to thrive. It won't even have the hint of a challenge toward righteousness because even the smallest amount of conviction is deemed as a judgment against a person. It's a gospel that coddles us while we continue to wallow in the miry clay of immoral behaviors and demoralizing attitudes.

Is that really the gospel? Is there any hope in that? Isn't it just more of the same treadmill mentality, continually walking in the same circles?

Don't we want to hear a word of truth that encourages us to rise up out of the muck and mire? Don't we want to listen to the voice of the Lord call us out of the darkness and translate us into His marvelous light?

What is the actual gospel? It is the good news: while in our destitute state as enemies of God, Christ died for us, paid the price of our sin and the ransom for our souls. We who believe are set free to walk in the power of His resurrection living as witnesses of His love, glory, and grace.

The gospel of victory declares we have been taken out of the hands of our captors, unleashed from the taskmaster and enemy of our soul, set free from the wages of sin and wrath of God, to walk in a manner that is worthy of Him. It is by His equipping power we can be made new, transformed into new creations, no longer bound by desires and sins.

The true gospel is one of increasing victory, and not just the success that Christ Himself experienced. But the success that we can and should experience in Christ. It challenges us to live higher, exercising and walking out in the equipping power of grace that continues to grant greater and greater conquests and triumphs. It's the hope of the gospel that we are being sanctified, being made progressively holier, as we continue to walk in pursuit of the heart and mind of God through our lives in every thought, attitude, action, and agenda. That the old man, that former sin-nature, would eventually not just come to surrender to the will of God, but be dead to the things of this flesh and the world.

We are called to live in a manner where our every gaze is upward, with a constant conviction. The pressing of the Holy Spirit will both correct and compel us ever upward toward victory.

Countless verses and examples throughout Scripture tell us we are more than conquerors (Romans 8:37), that we can do all things through Christ who strengthens us (Philippians 4:13), we are no longer slaves to sin (Rom 6:14), that we can stand against the devil's schemes (Ephesians 6:11), having been called out of darkness are brought into His marvelous light (1 Peter 2:9), and we are born of God and thereby we overcome the world (1 John 5:4).

God will not allow us to be tempted beyond what we can take (1 Corinthians 10:13). When evil comes, we can stand our ground (Ephesians 6:13), being refashioned into a new creation (2 Corinthians 5:17), delivering us from the power of darkness and translating us into the kingdom of His dear Son (Colossians 1:13-14). *"I beseech you therefore, brethren, by the mercies of God, that you present your bodies a living sacrifice, holy, acceptable to God, which is your reasonable service."* (Romans 12:1).

Yes, brokenness is part of our testimony, part of our walk, and part of our struggle. But it should be remorseful brokenness over our sin, and the repentance from it. If we live boastful, justifying our sin, which led us to our broken life, we are presenting a gospel of helplessness, imprint and powerless. The resurrection of Jesus empowers us to live in victory.

First Corinthians 5:17-20 plainly says that if Christ has not been raised from the dead, then our faith is futile and we are still in our sins. The resurrection of Christ is the hope of the gospel, that in Him, here and now we can have life and light while pursuing holiness and living victoriously. Though we may walk the rest of our life with a limp from an encounter and struggle with the Lord over an issue in our heart, if we hold on for Him to bless us, our very nature can be changed from that someone who undermines the things of God, to someone who flourishes in them.

Are we willing to be challenged by Grace?

The same *Power* that rose *Jesus* from the *dead,*

Lives in *you* who believe!

That Power puts angels to flight, defeats enemies, empowers you to overcome sin, comforts your heart, infuses you with compassion, ignites a passion for holiness, and equips you for every good work in Christ Jesus!

Is that *good news* or *what?*

Walk in it!

Extending Mercy

So speak and so do as those who will be judged by the law of liberty. For judgment is without mercy to the one who has shown no mercy. Mercy triumphs over judgment.
James 2:12-13

Extending mercy is a powerful thing. Here, Scripture is telling us that mercy triumphs over judgment. Like the wildcard in a game, it trumps anything else in our hand.

If someone commits a serious wrong against us, but is truly repentant, how are we to respond?

Mercy is born out of love and compassion, an act of forgiveness. Judgment is righteous, and pure and perfect when executed by God. It is born out of holiness and the purity and perfection of God, an act of holiness. Mercy is also holy, righteous and pure. It has the power to overcome judgments and triumph over them as an act of forgiveness. We no longer hold a grudge or debt over someone else.

Because Christ is both fully God and fully man, He alone was able to take on the sins of all mankind, the full wrath of God, and pay the debt we could never pay. Mercy is extended freely to all who believe, because the wrath of God against sin was satisfied in Christ's atonement. It merely needs to be accepted and lived in response to it. Doing so can radically change our life, our family, our community, our world…and the way we respond to others.

"The Spirit of the Lord is upon Me, Because He has anointed Me To preach the gospel to the poor; He has sent Me to heal the brokenhearted, To proclaim liberty to the captives And recovery of sight to the blind, To set at liberty those who are oppressed" (Luke 4:18).

There are times when judgement is necessary. It is an act of holiness, justice, and righteousness. It holds the unrepentant heart accountable for selfish actions. But mercy is to be extended to those with repentant hearts that ask for it, and bear the fruit of that repentance in their actions. Let's not withhold mercy.

Broken to Beautiful

But we have this treasure in earthen vessels, that the excellence of the power may be of God and not of us. We are hard-pressed on every side, yet not crushed; we are perplexed, but not in despair; persecuted, but not forsaken; struck down, but not destroyed...Therefore we do not lose heart. Even though our outward man is perishing, yet the inward man is being renewed day by day. For our light affliction, which is but for a moment, is working for us a far more exceeding and eternal weight of glory, while we do not look at the things which are seen, but at the things which are not seen. For the things which are seen are temporary, but the things which are not seen are eternal. 2 Cor 4:7-9, 16-18

Regardless of how broken you are, there is hope. The master can take your pieces and renew you.

I am amazed at how God takes so many things in our lives and repairs, restores, redeems and renews them. I recently created a message based on this Scripture and used an example of an ancient Japanese Fine Art form.

Kintsugi is a practice that is about 600 years old. Japanese masters would take a broken vessel, bowl, vase or cup and repair it with gold rather than discard it. This makes the container usable again, and rather than hide the scars, it accentuates them, embellishing them with gold, creating the piece, in most cases, more valuable than before.

In our consumer society, we are far too quick to throw away and upgrade, far too lazy to maintain and repair.

Unfortunately, that reaches across the American spectrum in more areas of life than we care to admit. It has invaded, our lives, workplace, families, and relationships, and it ultimately speaks of a considerable inequity in our character as a nation, society, and people.

Fortunately for us, God is not so quick to cast off, throw away or trash even a shattered vessel, like you and me.

So many cracks, so many broken pieces. Yet, He in vast love and desire to redeem what was lost, can work with our brokenness and make us not just like new. Better than new. Scars may remain, but they are merely a sign of victory, a remnant of what was meant for evil, that God in His mercy and grace was able to turn into good. He promises to be close to the brokenhearted, to bind up our wounds, and heal our hurts.

"And we know that all things work together for good to those who love God, to those who are the called according to His purpose...What then shall we say to these things? If God is for us, who can be against us?" (Romans 8:28-31).

Excuses, Excuses!

The sick man answered Him, "Sir, I have no man to put me into the pool when the water is stirred up; but while I am coming, another steps down before me."
John 5:7

Have you got excuses? Have you become weary in waiting? Do you want others to do the work for you? Or will you answer God's command? We are not alone in having excuses. Even Moses had them! He said he couldn't go to Pharaoh and speak for the Lord because he stuttered. So many throughout Scripture were fearful and raised excuses to justify their desire to escape out the back door or to defend their weariness, their doubt, or their complacency.

John 5:1-9 tells the fascinating story of the man lame for thirty-eight years who was healed by Jesus. There at the Pool of Bethesda (meaning: House of Mercy), Man's impotence met God's omnipotence. There God's commands became the man's enabling. "Get up, take your mat- Rise up and walk." It's where pardon and power make an impact and radically change a life. God's omnipotence is where excuses finally cease, and obedience in faith begins. It's where even someone with hope deferred and countless disappointments meet the source of life. It is at the House of Mercy we find help and hope. Jesus is the House of Mercy, the habitation and personification of Mercy.

"After this there was a feast of the Jews, and Jesus went up to Jerusalem. Now there is in Jerusalem by the Sheep Gate a pool, which is called in Hebrew, Bethesda, having five porches. In these lay a great multitude of sick people, blind, lame, paralyzed, waiting for the moving of the water. For an angel went down at a certain time into the pool and stirred up the water; then whoever stepped in first, after the stirring of the water, was made well of whatever disease he had. Now a certain man was there who had an infirmity thirty-eight years. When Jesus saw him lying there, and knew that he already had been in that condition a long time, He said to him, 'Do you want to be made well?' The sick man answered Him, 'Sir, I have no man to put me into the pool when the water is stirred up; but while I am coming, another steps down before me.' Jesus said to him, 'Rise, take up your bed and walk.' And immediately the man was made well, took up his bed, and walked (John 5:1-9a).

How tremendous that the Lord Jesus steps into the areas of our life where we have become weary of waiting, tired, old and left for dead by others, and then asks us if we want a fresh start.

Unfortunately for us, more often than not, we look at our past record of failures, errors, sins, problems, betrayals and the like instead of His prior history of mercy with all its many different types of healings, physically and spiritually.

Take up your mat. In other words, get up, get going, and get rid of that mat for good. Stop relying on it, wallowing in the feelings of despair, loneliness, and failure. Today is a new day to get going. Remember in the house of Mercy, we can come for new mercy every day.

No more excuses.

Get up. Go!

Consume Me, Lord

John answered, saying to all, "I indeed baptize you with water; but One mightier than I is coming, whose sandal strap I am not worthy to loose. He will baptize you with the Holy Spirit and fire.
Luke 3:16

In the Old Testament, the sacrifice and the wood were the consumables. The wood gathered was brought and laid under the altar then it was ignited by the presence of God. It was miraculous. It was to be a perpetual burning, with the constant addition of wood so that it never went out. That could be a significant task wandering around in a desert. I love looking at the Scriptures and seeing how so much of it is a foreshadowing of our own walk with the Lord.

Three things are needed for fire to exist.

- IGNITION (God's impact and confrontation in our life)
- FUEL (our actions, attitudes & agendas submitted & purged)
- OXYGEN (Holy Spirit to fan, breathe and infuse into the mix)

Without any one of these, the fire in us dies.

God being two parts of the equation, this leaves us as the variable. Are we willing to continually submit our lives to the Lord?

Being that GOD's heart is to consume us, those two are never in question. If the fire of God is not burning in our life, praying for more of it is not necessarily the answer. The ignition and oxygen already exist. He's waiting for the fuel, us.

So, what does it mean to be the fuel? What about us is consumable? We know that our lives are short, even at ninety years, it's a vapor in comparison to time. So, what other than years are consumable?

Often throughout Scriptures, the Lord equates mankind with trees, with wood. Our lives are to be a consumable before God, creating heat, fire, light. We are to live our lives, laying it down for others so they can eat and taste some of the goodness of God.

Additionally, as the Israelites would bring their beasts to the altar to sacrifice before the Lord, they were honoring God with their livelihood. Do we do that? Do we honor God with our lives? Does everything we do submit and surrender to His higher purpose? If not, there are a few beasts we may need to bring for slaughter.

Individual attitudes, actions and agendas we have, whether public or private, need to be killed and consumed by the fire. Things we have struggled with surrendering. Sins we have been hesitant to relinquish, long in justifying, and slow in seeing their harm.

What is the consumable entity in your life, the wood or the beast you need to present to God so that His holy fire can burn brightly in your life?

Deeply Rooted

As you therefore have received Christ Jesus the Lord, so walk in Him, rooted and built up in Him and established in the faith, as you have been taught, abounding in it with thanksgiving. Colossians 2:6,7

Several times, my husband and I have taken tours of vineyards. One time upstate New York on the rolling hills of the Finger Lake region, we went to one that deepened my walk with God.

Several vineyards in the area had sprinkler systems, but this one did not. When asked why, the answer caused me to stand there with my eyes and mouth wide open. Perhaps this is basic information to some, but for me, it pierced me to the core.

The guide said, "the reason we don't have sprinklers is that we want to force the roots to go deep. If we made it easy for the roots to obtain water with a sprinkler system, the roots would inadvertently stay close to the surface."

Someone asked, "Why would that be a bad thing seeing they would be watered by the sprinkler system?" The guide made mention of the years when there have been droughts and how the local government required them to stop watering, reserving the water for drinking and emergencies. During those times, the crops would not just fail to produce; they would die.

To lose the actual plant was worse than not reaping the harvest. By refusing to make it simple for the plant to have easy access to water, it forces the plants to work hard, to send roots down deep through the ground and the rocks in search of underground water sources. Seeking the springs and aquifers underground forces the plant to become strong and resilient, and help it find reliable water sources.

I was amazed at how simple that truth is for us. Indeed, there are times of refreshing in Christ where our water source comes from a daily resting, the morning and evening dew. Sometimes that is received from the preaching at a church service or the fellowship of believers in small groups, Bible studies, prayer meetings, podcasts or TV preachers. If that is all we rely on, our root system is shallow. There are times when we need to search the Word of God for ourselves, reading, studying, digging into commentaries, searching out things we don't understand or elude us.

These are the moments when our roots go deep in search of living waters.

The guide followed up by saying that during the times of drought, if the roots have found those underground water sources, even in a severe drought the vines can produce a crop. The grapes themselves will be smaller because of the lower water content, but that makes the sweetest and most expensive wines.

That speaks volumes to my spirit. We need to be a people who seek the Word of God for ourselves, digging deep for living waters. If we are willing to do this, even in times of drought, spiritually speaking, we will not be left without a reward in Christ.

It is sad when a fully grown and capable healthy child needs to be spoon-fed by their parents. If the child is never taught to cut their own meat or is drinking out of a bottle still at five years old, it shows how weak, that child actually is.

"of whom we have much to say, and hard to explain, since you have become dull of hearing. For though by this time you ought to be teachers, you need someone to teach you again the first principles of the [a]oracles of God; and you have come to need milk and not solid food. For everyone who partakes only of milk is unskilled in the word of righteousness, for he is a babe.". (Hebrews 5:11-13)

Lord, help us to grow, not to resent seeking out water on our own so that we can be deeply rooted, embracing the work, disciplined by Your precious Holy Spirit, that we might grow strong and thrive during the hard times of life.

The Vein of Gold

...the eyes of your understanding being enlightened; that you may know what is the hope of His calling, what are the riches of the glory of His inheritance in the saints...
Ephesians 1:18

I have often compared studying the Scriptures to working in an underground mine shaft.

Often reading through the Scriptures, I feel as though I am in a dark tunnel with a small amount of light to see. The view of previous understandings and revelation helps in the search, like a headlamp on a hard hat, but there is still labor on my part to find more.

With my spiritual pickax and tools in hand (pen, paper, reference books, commentaries, concordances, etc.), I start to chip away at the surface of the rock. I'll start in one corner or wall of the tunnel and just start chipping away.

There have been many times in preparing for a speaking engagement, a women's conference, or retreat where I am asked to bring a message. I pray and ask the Lord for wisdom, light and a message of gold that people will take away with them so that they can more fully grasp the riches of their relationship with Jesus Christ. I may start with an idea, and start digging through the Scriptures, looking for other references to match it and support it. As I chip away at my message, or what I am seeking to understand for myself, suddenly there is a glimmer of something more significant than I started with.

It is as if my pick ax just struck something that shines differently than the rock surrounding it. As I continue to investigate that thought, those Scriptures, those connections, a vein of revelation appears, the trail of heavenly gold. Something that so significantly challenges me, changes me and makes me more productive for understanding it.

Sometimes I find the vein of gold immediately, while other times I dig in the Scriptures for hours or days before there's a strike that's enriching.

When was the last time you went digging in the Word of God for yourself without the prompting or preaching of someone else?

Do you know someone that always seems to have an excellent grasp of the Scriptures, someone that gets excited when they share about what the Lord has shown them? Do you find yourself jealous spiritually, or feeling discouraged that you don't have that excitement? Then start digging. The gold is there to be found by you, but only if you do the digging yourself.

Don't know how? Then start with reading, asking questions, joining a Bible study, or buying some good commentaries and reference books that will be tools in your spiritual tool belt.

We have to consider the Word of God, even the aspects we've neglected, as a mine waiting to unearth the riches. The riches will not be made manifest unless we get in there ourselves.

Nuggets of spiritual gold are tucked within the walls of the Bible. So much of the riches of Christ are concealed in the Old Testament passages.

Jesus equated Himself, His death, and resurrection to Jonah in the belly of the whale. He related the bronze serpent on the pole and its ability to break the power of the serpent's bite, to His death on the cross and belief in Him that destroys the power of sin. At the beginning of Jesus' ministry, He read from the book of Isaiah and told the listeners that it was fulfilled in their hearing. He likened the Temple of God, its destruction and rebuilding to His own flesh. In one of the most significant discussions with two followers on the road to the town of Emmaus, Jesus started with the writings of Moses and showed how He fulfilled them.

Imagine how every instance of Old Testament truth would have exploded open with life eternal!

New Testament or Old, all of the Scriptures are powerful and enriching. Start digging and find the nuggets of holy ore for yourself.

"The heart of the prudent acquires knowledge, And the ear of the wise seeks knowledge" (Proverbs 18:15).

Seeing Things Far Off

These all died in faith, not having received the promises, but having seen them afar off were assured of them, embraced them and confessed that they were strangers and pilgrims on the earth...And all these, having obtained a good testimony through faith, did not receive the promise, God having provided something better for us, that they should not be made perfect apart from us.
Hebrews 11:13, 39-40

Chapter 11 of Hebrews displays many heroes of the faith. People like Abraham, Moses, Isaac, those crossing the Red Sea, others watched the walls of Jericho fall. Women who saw their dead raised to life, while others were not as fortunate. Some wandered living in deserts, mountains, caves, some destitute, mistreated, imprisoned, killed for their faith. It is a hard chapter to ponder.

Interestingly, the last portion of the Scripture shows that their testimony is not apart from us. Those saints are actually linked to our testimony, a line of connection, a foundation which we are built upon. Our faith helps to give their faith a fuller meaning and purpose, something they could not see in their own time.

Have you known someone who has had a difficult life, trials that seemed daunting, and yet they continued to move forward in Christ? Perhaps they are quiet, maybe they are bold.

I knew one such woman. Her name was Ida Ward. She was
born in the deep south September of 1900. This young girl was
married off to a friend of her father, 20 years her senior. Within
a year of getting married, she was pregnant and had twin girls.
At a few months old, one of the twins died. At that point, her
husband left her, and she had to raise her daughter alone.

She became a low-paid worker in the cotton fields of Louisiana.
Bartering to make ends meet, she found herself fighting poverty
constantly. Years later, her daughter married and then had her
own little girl. They moved around from state to state with the
Air Force. Ida was alone now, caring for her very aged mother.
Eventually, she came to live with her daughter, son-in-law, and
granddaughter in a 19-foot trailer for several years. Her life was
one with real heartbreak and real struggles, but none overcame
her genuine faith. She always looked to the Lord and pointed
others toward him as well. She poured what and when she could
into her granddaughter who when she got older, married and
started having her own children.

Ida never married again.

As time passed, her granddaughter and great-grandchildren
settled in New York. She had opportunities to share with them
not just her love, but her faith.

One year, two of Ida's great-granddaughters, my sister and I,
then in our 20's, visited her during a vacation in Arkansas. We
had extensive talks with "Mama Ward," and we were able to

glean from her Godly wisdom as she shared her love of the Lord with us.

She shared how she longed to see her husband soon and then turned and said, "You know I mean the Lord. He has been a husband to me all these years." She turned at one point and said, "I prayed for you girls before you were even born."

A few years later, Ida passed away and finally got to meet the Lover of her soul. She didn't get to see all that the family would become, but she could rest knowing that her family was being kept by the Lord. By this time, her granddaughter that she lived with, my mother, had become a woman of prayer and ministry and had three children, all of which are in ministry, as are a couple of her great-great-grandchildren.

What a beautiful and precious legacy. Ida imparted Christ. He grew in the lives of those she loved and prayed for. She left a legacy of ministry and impacted the kingdom of God, to the third and fourth generation after her.

I see her as one similar to some of those in Hebrews 11. Despite of all her hardship, she continued steadfast in the faith, paving the way for generations after her to follow. I am eternally grateful. I have received a great blessing, and yet she gets a great reward for having paved the way, a woman of faith.

Who has impacted your life?
Whose life can you impact, perhaps generations from now?
Maybe you are the start of such a lineage!

Fighting Giants

Yet it was I who destroyed the Amorite before them, Whose height was like the height of the cedars, And he was as strong as the oaks; Yet I destroyed his fruit above And his roots beneath. Also it was I who brought you up from the land of Egypt, And led you forty years through the wilderness, To possess the land of the Amorite.
Amos 2:9,10

A year after God delivered the Israelites from the bondage of Egypt, He brought them to the border of the Promised Land. It wasn't without its challenges, but He would secure them if they would obey and believe.

You can read all about the fear that took hold of their hearts when they were given the ability to spy out the land. They saw that the area was lush and green, with fruit abounding, a land of flowing with milk and honey. *Yet*, the inhabitants were *huge*! They were giant warriors, and the Israelites felt inferior, inadequate, and incapable of conquering them. They said, "We are like grasshoppers" in comparison to their size.

Their lack of faith, and ultimately their rebellion, required them to wander around the desert for forty years before they would have another opportunity to take the land God wanted to give them.

They trusted their eyes more than their God, who I might add, proved with many immeasurable acts, starting with the ten plagues in Egypt of His power to conquer enemies. They refused to trust God; in fact, they were going to stone to death not just the two spies that wanted to take the land, but Moses and Aaron as well.

Sometimes we read this, with our 20/20 vision and ask, "Why wouldn't they trust God?" But think about it. How many times have you encountered a giant in your life and been too afraid to conquer?

I've overcome and fought against a few giants in my life but ran from the conflict at first before God cornered me in situations where I had little or no choice but to deal with it.

In 1 Samuel 17, King Saul's entire army was terrified. They were mocked for forty days by a giant named Goliath. A young shepherd boy named David had brought his older brothers' provisions for the battle. When he heard the giant mock God and His people, he was indignant! Having been trained in the field of protection against wolves, bears, and lions; he felt he could fight this unholy giant. His brothers and the king gave him some flack, but eventually he fought the giant, and ended up cutting off Goliath's head.

His eyes and his heart were fixed on the Lord God Almighty, the One in whom he found not just his strength and courage, but his hope and his future.

If we focus our eyes on the Lord, and all that He seeks to accomplish in and through us, for us and for our future, we will trust Him with the giants we face.

Do you have some giants that intimidate or control you, things you can't break free from? Trust the Lord and move out to battle in His strength, trusting His power for you. He will equip you for the battle and bring the giants to the ground.

Raw Clay in His Hands

And the vessel that he made of clay was marred in the hand of the potter; so he made it again into another vessel, as it seemed good to the potter to make. Then the word of the Lord came to me, saying: "O house of Israel, can I not do with you as this potter?" says the Lord. "Look, as the clay is in the potter's hand, so are you in My hand, O house of Israel!"
Jeremiah 18:4-6

Ever feel so discouraged that you wonder if God can use you? Ever feel like you have made so many mistakes that you're too damaged to be a vessel for God's glory? Ever wonder what possible future you could have after all the messes you've been in, and how they have ruined your life?

You are not alone. Many of the prophets and characters in the history of Israel wondered the same thing.

Abraham lied about his wife to protect his own life, and slept with his wife's handmaiden to have a child, creating chaos in his family.

Jacob tricked his brother out of his birthright and then deceived his father so that he could obtain the final inheritance for himself.

Joseph boasted to his ten older brothers about dreams he had about ruling over them.

Moses killed someone, thinking it would help set someone else free.

David forced himself on the wife of one of his high-ranking officials and then had him killed when David found out she was pregnant.

That's just a small list of the heavy hitters, but there are many, many more. The point is not that they made significant blunders, even broke several of the Ten Commandments, but that they were repentant, and they submitted to God. In return, He forgave them and then used them in His plan of redemption.

They weren't dry hard clay, they were soft and pliable clay in God's hands., clay that God could then refashion after it became flawed, marred, broken.

This is the hope of the gospel of Jesus Christ. It is the mercy of God to take your mistakes, your sinful past, those blunders and remold you into the image He determines for you. But this requires a pliable heart, one that has gone through the process of having the debris removed from the clay of your life, pounded and massaged out the grit and sand, those fine things hidden with the clay that could comprise the integrity of the vessel He seeks to create of you.

Will you allow the Lord to sift you, sort through your life, surrendering it all to His hand?

If so, there is only hope for you. That should give your heart a new song and new purpose.

Be Still

But when the grain ripens, immediately he puts in the sickle,
because the harvest has come.
Mark 4:29

***

Be still, and know that I am God; I will be exalted among the
nations, I will be exalted in the earth!
Psalm 46:10

In both of these situations, it is a powerful and loud rebuke that gets the attention and causes a sudden halt to the escalating chaos.

Have you ever been in a situation where several people are clamoring, prodding, questioning, accusing, crying and interfering the same time; where the person in charge was so distracted, they couldn't hear themselves much less take control of the situation? What usually happens? A loud bullhorn, hand clap, slamming of a gavel, or a sudden loud shout is needed to cut through the noise to get all attention fixed on one spot, and then direct them into order.

Be still! Whether it is the Lord reprimanding the nations and their strife against each other or Him, or the Lord rebuking the wind and the waves to calm a storm, which seemed to cause chaos and fear to overtake the hearts of his disciples.

Sometimes we hear the Scripture of Psalm 46:10, "Be still and know that I am God." And get this warm fuzzy feeling as if we are being hugged by God.

I wonder, though: do we see that in both instances, it was a stern, bold, even loud, forceful rebuke to the chaos? Have we have gotten caught up such chaos? Are voices raging in our heads and terrifying our hearts? Do we question God's care for us, His love, His provision and protection?

It's when God interjects His authority into a chaotic situation that we can be suddenly struck with awe. In those moments when He intervenes, we see Him in all power and authority. Shocked by glory and provision, we are humbled. We may even find ourselves asking, "Who is that even the wind and waves obey Him?"

Are there situations at your job, in your family, at church, with friends, where God needs to intervene? Perhaps there are injustices, false accusations, rumors, plans or malicious entanglements that need to be silenced. Pray for His shout.

Give God room to exercise His authority and then get out of His way. Listen for the Lord and when you see the storm quelled you too, will be amazed and know He is God.

Hassle or Honor?

Then they came to Him, bringing a paralytic who was carried by four men. And when they could not come near Him because of the crowd, they uncovered the roof where He was. So when they had broken through, they let down the bed on which the paralytic was lying.
Mark 2:3, 4

Imagine the scene: Jesus is at *your* house speaking. News of His miracles have been running in the streets, creating the most exciting buzz for days, and now He is at your home!

The place is packed. I mean, *full*. People are squeezing into every conceivable corner and crevice. Everyone is pressed up against a wall or other individuals, sitting on the chairs, the tables, the floor, in doorways. It is jammed. Everyone is there. The neighbors, the family, and friends, co-workers, political and religious leaders…everyone!

It's so crowded that people are blocking the doors and windows, overflowing into the yard and street, all trying to listen in and see what is going on. It's quiet inside, and people are intently listening to what Jesus has to say. It's a spectacle.

What do you do? I've had a crowd or two at my house, and my concern is always for the cesspool, since at one party, with only forty people it overflowed. Not fun. It was a hassle and had an expensive outcome. I imagine I might be thinking along those lines in this situation.

Here, it is so crowded that a few latecomers, four men carrying their paralytic friend on a cot, make their way up to the roof, and start to dig through the mud and straw to create a hole large enough to lower their friend down to Jesus.

Imagine the homeowner. Perhaps for a while, he has no idea of what is happening since the roof would be thick with mud, straw, and wood. Eventually, it would become evident as small pieces of debris started to fall down in front of Jesus as He was speaking. What would the homeowner do? Perhaps, with the home so crammed, he could do nothing but watch like everyone else. Then to see a man's hand pop through, and enlarge the whole, and eventually some feet and then the whole body of this paralyzed man lowered to the floor!

As the story goes, that man was eventually healed, and he walked away. Finally, the crowds left, and life in the home went back to normal. But what about that hole? Who's responsible? Who's going to fix that?

I'm sure after the crowds all left, there was a considerable amount of cleaning, reorganizing and some significant repairs. How do you think that homeowner felt? Was he upset by the inconvenience making his home available to the Lord created? Was he bothered with the cost he and his family have incurred? What about the physical energy he had to expend to repair his roof? Was it a hassle or an honor?

Often times in ministry, there is *no* paycheck. Things we do cost us! Is it a hassle or an honor? Do we seek to be reimbursed? Or do we count it a privilege to participate in the kingdom of God?

I've seen so many people who start out volunteering suddenly require compensation for their service. People who at first seem to be so excited to serve suddenly are squabbling over pennies, rather than taking in the wonder of helping and making available their lives for the Lord's use.

How about you? Are you willing to be inconvenienced for the Kingdom? Are you ready to let it cost you, whether time, comfort, energy or finances?

Would it be a hassle or an honor?

To Infinity and Beyond

Great is our Lord, and mighty in power;
His understanding is infinite.
Psalm 147:5

Can't you just hear Buzz Lightyear saying that as he stands ready for blast off?

It's a tremendous thought going into the unknown, where few have tread. All who go are awestruck with wonder.

We have that kind of journey in Christ. God is infinite! Unfathomable! Unsearchable!

Yet, this eternal God wants us to come close and learn of Him. To learn of His character, attributes, knowledge, wisdom, love, compassion.

He is living, eternal, and beyond our knowing fully. Yet, He is at the same time personal and intimately acquainted with us.

Have you not known? Have you not heard? The everlasting God, the Lord, The Creator of the ends of the earth, Neither faints nor is weary. His understanding is unsearchable (Isaiah 40:28).

I say all this just because I had a pleasant conversation with a new believer recently. One of her regrets was, "I've wasted so much time" and "I've got so much to learn, I'll never catch up."

People have looked at me in comparison and felt inadequate in their own walk. Not realizing that I feel that way standing next to some that I know.

God has shown me this paradox: though someone may know more about God that we do, they still have just as much to learn How can that be?

God is eternal: no beginning, no end. There is no ability to know all about Him. Whether you are a Billy Graham or a newly saved person, we all have just as much to learn about God!

Get it? When I finally realized this, it was a huge relief. It didn't give me the opportunity to get lazy and stop growing. Instead, it gave me more reason to reach for Him. No matter how much someone knows about God, she has just as much to learn as someone new to the faith, because God is infinite and eternal.

If you are feeling low in comparison, as long as you are on the move toward God, don't fret it. Forward motion is great. Don't stagnate in your walk of faith. Get going, and move forward in the knowledge, wisdom and experience with God through prayer, reading, studying, serving, and submitting to Him.

The Potter's Wheel

But now, O Lord, You are our Father; We are the clay, and You our potter; And all we are the work of Your hand.
Isaiah 64:8

Ever feel like a wet mess of mud—full of debris, seemingly unusable? Ever feel like your life is spinning so fast you could be thrown against a wall?

Clay has so many interesting properties. Gathered from hillsides, river banks or bogs, it is used to make beautiful and useful pieces of pottery or porcelain. But there is a process that the clay must first go through to be made ready for the potter. It is beaten and rolled, then all the impurities are worked out of it, the debris, dead plant materials, sand, pebbles, broken fragments of bone, metal and more. The clay is then placed on a potter's spinning wheel and worked into a shape. Once the shape is successfully completed it is placed in a fire and hardened.

Clay doesn't seem to have much value to you and me, but to a potter, it's wonderful. He sees the value of the clay while it is in its messy environment. He has a vision for it, for what it will become, what he wants to make before he even goes on the hunt for the clay.

He is willing to work the clay, to take the time necessary to work out all the impurities that could damage the end product. He never gives up on the clay.

Eventually, it becomes a vessel of honor, something his loving hands have worked into a masterpiece.

Second Corinthians 4:7 tells us, *"But we have this treasure in earthen vessels, that the excellence of the power may be of God and not of us."*

Trust the Potter's hands. He has a vision for your life, and there is a process in fulfilling that vision. Some of the process is slow, some painful, some redundant, but if we try to rush it, or reject the process, we cannot fulfill the purpose the master has for us.

Pray in faith for yourself, and for those you love going through difficulties...

As long as you are in His Hands, even when you feel like your life is spinning, trust Him.

He's got you!

Colors of Splendor

Now for the house of my God I have prepared with all my might: gold for things to be made of gold, silver for things of silver, bronze for things of bronze, iron for things of iron, wood for things of wood, onyx stones, stones to be set, glistening stones of various colors, all kinds of precious stones, and marble slabs in abundance.
1 Chronicles 29:2

Who doesn't get excited about precious and semi-precious stones? If you ever get a chance to go to the Museum of Natural History in New York City, don't miss the Minerals Exhibit. There is a tremendous amount of gorgeous large stones, diamonds, rubies, emeralds, tourmalines and so many more. Those stones are all so beautiful, with their different sizes, shapes and colors.

The Scriptures mention these crystals several times: as gifts given by foreign kings to Solomon, in the Ephod worn by the High Priest, in the temple walls, and the foundations stones of the New Jerusalem. In fact, believers are similarly linked to them when Peter says we are "living stones".
Imagine all the colors. What a beautiful sight, what glorious splendor! It got me searching out some interesting aspects of these crystals and one in particular that fascinated me was their color variations.

Do you know what makes them so gloriously colorful?

I pondered the question, and in finding the answer, was amazed at how it speaks of you and me.

Color is determined by the trace elements, the mineral deposits...essentially, the contaminants and impurities. The nature of the visible light spectrum, along with the different impurities and/or inclusions, determines the color of each unique gemstone.

Read that again: the light, as it passes through the structure, hits the small residual impurities and inclusions and causes the light to display different colors.

None of us comes to Christ perfect. We all come with impure hearts, issues, problems and sins. Those impurities, those inclusions, get surrendered to the Lord, and His forgiveness passes His Light through them, displaying a glorious color, a precious site of redemption, restoration, and renewal. Those things in our past, help to color us in Christ.

Your imperfections, those trace elements of life, deposits, and contaminants, color you. He eventually can take us as stones gathered from the ground. He cuts us, He polishes and purposes the precious colored stones for glory as He sets us into a crown all His own.

Be encouraged: we are not all the same stone, color or size...not the same personality or passions, but in Christ, we are all *His*...

Let Him set you in His crown.

Give Liberally!

There is one who scatters, yet increases more; And there is one who withholds more than is right, But it leads to poverty. The generous soul will be made rich, And he who waters will also be watered himself.
Proverbs 11:24-25

Is it possible to live in a place where we lavish on others out of the abundance of God's work in our heart? Can we generously pour out on others an overwhelming flow of compassion, care, love, goodness, and kindness, in the face of insult, disapproval or rejection?

One Sunday, I got to pray with a woman feeling insecure, discouraged and disapproved of by coworkers. It was severely impacting her. Discouragement always does. We prayed.

Discouragement comes in when we are poorly positioned. Often when we compare ourselves to others instead of believing what Christ says of us. Sometimes discouragement comes when we have expectations of others that aren't met.

Don't look for the approval, the affirmation, or the response from someone who won't or can't give it. When we don't get it, then we feel hurt as if stolen from, as if they knocked us down and took something from us. Instead, recognize that our authority, our value, our call forward, is from Christ, our wonder, faith, purpose, and value is found in Him. That will cause us to walk in power others can't rattle. It will empower and equip us to react opposite of what the world would expect.

Instead, it will give us joy and infuses us the ability to lavish on them goodness they cannot contain, or return. Then, because it's within our authority to give, it's not something that can be taken. Instead, we choose to give, lavishly; then, we are in the seat of power and authority, not them.

When we are willing to be generous with mercy, compassion, forgiveness or grace, we are in a blessed state, a proper position of authority.

This doesn't mean we don't have boundaries, that we neglect to recognize or rebuke sin, that we are dismissive of lousy behavior and incorrect beliefs, or we can't be hurt by words or glances. It only means we take authority over it and operate out of the fruit of the Spirit. Instead, we firmly position ourselves in His love which can then overflow out of us with the same compassion Jesus had for us.

Instead of being under them, longing for something from them, we rise above the fray and give to them in spite of merit. I think we see that in Christ's example.

Power of the Cross

Having disarmed principalities and powers, He made a public spectacle of them, triumphing over them in it.
Colossians 2:15

Do we actually see the cross as powerful?

How powerful?

I was talking with a friend recently about Good Friday. And how most services are, well, morbid. I understand that we should consider the events of that day, how they brought on Jesus' flesh the wrath of us all. I understand that in remembering the physical activities of that day, we come to see the depth of His love. But could it be we focus so much on what happened to the physical body of Jesus, we neglect to see the spiritual power and ramifications the cross brought forth?

If all we do is focus on the physical pain Jesus endured, are we seeing beyond the veil of His flesh to what impact it ultimately had?

When we leave a Good Friday service, does it feel like we just lost a friend at a funeral, or are we transfixed with great joy at what the cross accomplished?

I understand Jesus endured incredible torture and physical pain, humiliation, mutilation, and rejection. I know that He died an absolutely gruesome and horrific death. These are all important to understand and have a real grasp of. The timelines, the corrupt courts, and accusations. The rejections, but let us also recognize that the power of the cross is so much more than what happened to Jesus' physical body.

Do we walk away transformed and empowered by it or merely emotionally moved or guilted by it?

Certainly, the death and blood of Christ are referred to through Scripture, but the sense of morbidity is not attached to it. Those Scriptures speak in context with the *power* of the *cross*, its purpose and what it secured.

What really happened? Was it just a horrific scene? Or can we get a glimpse and peer into eternity, with spiritual eyes to see all that was accomplished at the cross.

Here are a few indicators that something deeper, unseen, dynamic, celestial, explosive, spiritual and radical took place:

- The sky went black at midday for three hours. That's 180 minutes. This was no solar eclipse!
- The rocks split, and there was a massive earthquake!
- The thirty-foot-high, six-inch thick veil that separated all men from the presence of God in the Temple was ripped to shreds!

This terrified everyone!

The heavens, the earth, and the religious order were experiencing something so powerful that they were tearing apart at the seams! Not since God spoke and said, "Let there be light" had anything this explosive happened in the universe.

The debt owed for sin was paid in full! Satan was made a public spectacle because Christ canceled all transgressions and ordinances by nailing them to the cross!

The separation of men from God was removed, and the separation among men from each other was removed!

Sin was conquered at the cross. The reconciliation and peace between God and mankind was restored. The love of God for His creation was displayed in the greatest sacrifice!

He prepared a way for us to be set free and thereby restored order to the universe! The Word of God, Jesus, created order from chaos once again. He redeemed the creation He made in His own image and vanquished the enemy of mankind.

Mankind can be released from the shackles and bondage of slavery to sin, through Jesus Christ. We are released from the authority of sin and death if we will believe and follow after the Lord.

It is at the cross that Christ canceled the written code and ordinances against us and removed it, creating a new and better covenant, one not kept by the blood of animals, but secured by His own son, Jesus Christ.

We are now invited into the Most Holy Place, the very throne room of God where we can receive mercy and grace in times of need. The door that was once closed is now open forever to those who would come.

Unmerited forgiveness is given to cover our overwhelming debt. Righteousness and blamelessness are imputed to us who were once wretched and guilty. Jesus blood secured our safety from the angel of death. The ransom has been paid with it. We were washed white and clean with it and justified before God by it.

He snatched the keys of hell and death from the devil's grasp and conquered them both. The bite and curse of the deadly serpent has been reversed, and we are healed.

That is explosive, and I haven't even looked at the empty tomb yet!

Seeing and recognizing these truths puts an exclamation point on the resurrection of Jesus. It is in His power and authority to make all these changes in the universe. This makes me all the more humble, all the more rejoicing, all the more surrendering of my sinful heart. Knowing that Resurrection Power is now available for those who are willing to live for Him, is mind blowing!

That is some of the power of the cross!

He Is, I AM

Jesus said to them, "Most assuredly, I say to you, before Abraham was, I AM." John 8:58

***

Now when He said to them, "I am He," they drew back and fell to the ground. John 18:6

God declared His name to Moses as, "I AM that I AM." Throughout Scripture, it becomes clear that Jesus is God. In the two Scripture referenced above, He equated Himself with God. In reading the Scriptures, we learn of the multi-faceted image of God, much like a diamond being turned in the light and see the manifold glory of God.

He is the first and the last, the alpha and omega, the beginning and the end. He is ever true, ever holy, everlasting, compassionate, omnipotent, the creator of all things.

He is our all-powerful redeemer, equipper, encourager, and friend. He engages the outcast, brings close those who feel afar off. He is the healer of the hurting, lifter of the head, wiper away of every tear, the counter of every hair and the bestower of every blessing.

By His Spirit, He convicts the world of sin and judgment. He leads, He guides, He corrects, He teaches, and He instructs, He is an advocate before the father, He is the great High Priest, our fortress of refuge, the Bright and Morning Star.

He is the one through whom all creation- seen and unseen were brought forth. His word upholds all things. His authority is unparalleled, unmatched, unsuppressed. It cannot be thwarted by any number of armies or demons.

All of creation obeys His voice.

When He speaks, the mountains quake, the beasts of the field bring forth their young, and storms are commissioned or silenced. Mountains herald His majesty and valleys display his humility.

His wisdom is unsearchable, His peace unfathomable, his Glory all wonderful,

He is our Wonderful Counselor, Everlasting Father, King of Kings, Lord of Lords and Prince of Peace.
He is the restorer of the broken places, the desire of the nations, the satisfier of every soul, the light of the world.

He is the living water, the bread of life, and the salt of the earth. He is exalted above all gods, His name is above every other name, it alone provides salvation to the lost, help for the hurting, hope for the hopeless, a future and a purpose.

HE is I AM!

Though He is God, He emptied himself, becoming a man and the perfect sinless substitute sacrifice to atoned for every debt. He paid for every transgression and obliterates every account on the cross.

Jesus received all the wrath of God for sin, yours and mine.
He was tortured, tormented, beaten battered and bruised
and on that cross He Died.

Yet it was there and then, that
 the rocks broke open and the earth shook violently.
The Sky went black for 3 hours at midday.
He tore the veil of the temple from top to bottom with His
invisible hands as if to say,

I am the one who sets the captives free,
I am the one who removes the separation between YOU & ME.
I cancel every written code with all its regulations and
ordinances. I have nailed it all to My tree!
He has canceled the power of sin and death forever.
He has disarmed all powers and principalities that day.
He made a public spectacle of the devil and triumphed over him
at HIS cross.

He is the retriever of the keys of Hell and death
Vanquishing all His enemies!

On the Third day - He Rose up to prove beyond any measure of
any doubt that:
He IS the Resurrection, the Way, the Truth and the Life,
He is both the Lion and the Lamb.
He WAS, He IS and FOREVER shall BE.

HE is I AM!

Listen to the music and see other aspects of this amazing ministry, click the link below:

www.GraciousVine.com

Joanna's other books include:

- *Creation to Christ: Timelines and Charts*

- *Romans: A Workbook Study*

- *Adam Chronicles: Journal of the First Man* (Novel)

- *God's Blueprint: Prophetically Drafted in the Tabernacle of Moses*

All can be purchased in book or pdf form from:

http://www.lulu.com/spotlight/joannafruhauf

Each devotion was just one point in a message delivered by Joanna at either a women's event, church service, retreat or conference. Consider hosting Joanna for your next event. For booking information:

www.GraciousVine.com

GraciousVine@gmail.com

God's Blueprint: Prophetically Drafted in the Tabernacle of Moses

By Joanna Fruhauf

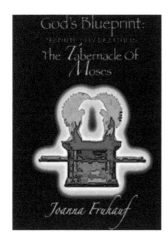

Prophetically drafted within the Tabernacle of Moses is a blueprint of glorious types and shadows. They represent the earthly walk of Jesus Christ, His ministry and His powerful work of Redemption. In addition to this there is a host of symbolism regarding our own personal walk with Christ, the calling of God through ministry and our maturing faith in Him.

Certainly this book is not exhaustive, though it is intense and full from cover to cover with various revelations, and understandings that have been gleaned from trusted writers, this century and previous ones as well as personal learnings from the scriptures through the Holy Spirit. Everyone whether a new or seasoned christian will have much to gain from its pages.

This is a must read!

The Adam Chronicles: Journal of the First Man

By Joanna Fruhauf

View this Author's Spotlight

eBook (PDF), 188 Pages ★★★☆☆ (1 Ratings)

Price: $12.95

This novel, journals Adam's thoughts and emotions as he may have dealt with various situations and events in his life following the fall into sin. Starting on that dreadful day, we follow Adam through His life through various traumas and joys. We become witnesses to the stories as they may have played out.

During Adam's 930 year life span, His single hope is in the promised 'Seed' that will come and restore all things to their previous state.

For this He hopes and focuses on.

Creation to Christ

By Joanna Fruhauf

eBook (PDF), 23 Pages ☆☆☆☆☆   This item has not been rated yet

Price: $9.95

This booklet has a total of 23 different charts and or timelines that will help you traverse through the scriptures from Genesis and to the time of Jesus Birth, Starting with an overview of the Bible's Books and their chronological placement this booklet touches on the Patriarchs, the Exodus, the Wanderings, The Tabernacle, the Kings of Israel, and the Subsequent world powers from Babylon to the Roman Empire as seen in the Visions of Daniel.

Excellent source for teaching and personal study.

ROMANS: A Study of God's Righteousness

By Joanna Fruhauf

eBook (PDF), 55 Pages ☆☆☆☆☆   This item has not been rated yet

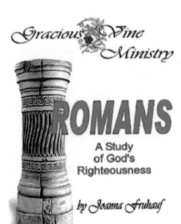

Price: $10.00

This is a Wonderful Study of the Righteousness of God in Contrast to man's. Rather than a Theological study, this one will excite and engage you in the powerful truths and their transforming impact on your life, practically, personally and spiritually!